People do not decide to become extraordinary.
They decide to accomplish extraordinary things.

Sir Edmund Hillary

ADVENTURE LIVES HERE!

MY JOURNEY TO ADVENTURE
AND
TAKING YOU WITH ME;
PACK YOUR BAG!

CAM JAMES

echo))
BOOKS

First Published in 2022 by Echo Books

Echo Books is an imprint of Superscript Publishing Pty Ltd, ABN 76 644 812 395

Registered Office: Suite 401, 140 Bourke St, Melbourne, VIC, 3000

www.echobooks.com.au

Copyright ©Cam James

Creator: Cam James

Title: Adventure Lives Here, My journey to adventure and
taking you with me; pack your bag!

ISBN: 978-1-922603-07-4 (paperback)

A catalogue record for this book is available from the National Library of Australia

Book layout and design by Peter Gamble, Canberra.
Set in Garamond Premier Pro Display, 12/17 and/Trajan Pro3 .

www.echobooks.com.au

CONTENTS

Prologue	vii
The standard has been set	1
Commencing the adventure journey	9
Simple choices made difficult	15
Being inculcated with a set of values	23
It's not a job, it's an adventure	37
Tough times never last, tough people do	47
The desert is your friend	65
New directions	79
Getting comfortable being uncomfortable	89
What doesn't kill you makes you stronger	97
Why I love Kokoda	125
100% World Wide Adventures	139
Looking at the top of the world	147
Building the opportunity door	167
Great Southern Land	175
The family	193
The future	205

*Nick looked at the obstacle and completed his 'walk-through' as I sat in the car
taking this photo between reading emails.
As he stepped back into the car he said, 'I think we're good.'*

PROLOGUE

It's hard for me to pass blame when I think of the words I'd used just a matter of hours earlier. Encouraging, daring, tempting or just plain egging on could be some of the ways you might describe my comments to my mate and business partner Nick, as we sat in our brand-new car looking at a mud hole.

With the light of day now quickly fading into the night sky, I shifted my position under the car that now sat on a 45-degree angle bogged to the sump.

Nick had been talking to me as I dug at the mud under the car with a stick, though my head being under the car muffled his voice. Having heard him stop talking, I was too focussed to note the conversation he was now beginning to have on his phone. Covered from head to bare foot in the thickest black watery mud imaginable, I climbed out from my muddy cocoon, hearing a man on the other end of the phone saying, 'you're where? You want to go where? And when do you want this? Oh man, that's going to cost you.'

Clearing the edge of the vehicle, I looked up to see Nick staring at me with laser focus, 'I need you to look at me, I have made the call, we're getting a cab, if we don't go now, you'll dig all night.' I laughed—maybe he knew me better than I realised. He was right, I would have dug all night or at least until I had the car out of this mess.

Many hours earlier, Nick and I had been driving the back roads of the Victorian coast. We were conducting a final reconnaissance mission in search of emergency access gates. With a trek along the Great Ocean Walk beginning in a matter of days, we'd been assessing the condition of the dirt access routes to ensure they were not only passable in the event that we had to conduct an emergency, but they would afford a level of comfort to a potentially injured client. These are the lengths we take to maintain the safety and comfort of our 'Adventurers,' the title afforded to our clients. Not only do we want to know the routes to and from every access point, we also want to know their condition.

On this day, we were in our new vehicle—a Mitsubishi Triton, the second in our fleet. This was not the primary vehicle used for an evacuation, that was a Toyota Troop Carrier, the Troopy. The positive of being in the Triton was that it was less suitable to the conditions we faced. This meant that in the event we were able to drive all areas in this car, there would be absolutely no issues when the Troopy was being utilised, it's better suited to the conditions and if required, is easier to recover.

The Troopy also had recovery gear, something the Triton lacked this day—we'd yet to fit it out. It was also the very thing we currently needed more than anything.

The Triton hadn't been modified in any way—it was straight off the showroom floor. The tyres, wheels and shock absorbers were 'stock', not the after-market items required to negotiate a road like this.

Having checked all but one route, Nick and I drove down a tight road; we were about as far away from our home base as you could be. It was mid-afternoon when we came to a section of trail that was close to three to four times the width of any section we'd previously passed. This section was littered with water-filled holes. I was alarmed—Nick not so much.

Nick said he thought we could get through it. I happened to be on my phone replying to an email; I looked at him and said 'sweet, get out and have a look, do a walk-through'.

I could see Nick looking at the conditions, assessing the best way through the water-filled holes. As far as I could tell, we were left with two options—one, have a crack at making it, or two, turn around and head back the way we came. Option two would have us return the following day in the Troopy to assess this section of road. Nick was keen to have a go now.

Nick returned to the car and said, 'I think we're good'. To me it was a clear 'no', but I went with it, almost encouraging him and laughing at the preposterousness of the idea. I said, 'we're over 100km from home, we have no recovery gear, we're in a brand-new car that has no after-market equipment with stock tyres, we're wearing thongs (flip flops)—what could go wrong?' Nick's excitement was infectious—my mind had been changed; I was now all in too!

I suggested we go live on Facebook and show our community what we faced. When the screen told me we were recording and people could see us, I asked the initial few viewers what they thought of our predicament, turning the camera so they too could see what we could. It's at this point from the comfort of their home, office or wherever these people were that they too seemed excited at the chance of an adventure; it was also apparent that they cared not if we bogged the vehicle. I would liken it to a situation where you can see something bad about to happen and almost will it. 'You can do it' they encouraged, not that we needed more encouragement, we were pumped to have a go. I asked Nick what chances of success he gave us as the wheels began to turn from the hard road to mud—alarmed at his reply of 30%.

It's a funny thing when you are live on social media and you feel the car start to roll to a side. I recall profanity coming from Nick as we hit the first bump, I remember the windscreen rising and falling in front of my face and I recall the car aggressively tipping to the right and then tipping even more as we came to a screaming halt. Facebook was a wall of laughing faces flowing up the screen in front of me. Uncontrollably laughing almost with fear, I quickly said, 'I have to go' and ended the broadcast, water began pouring through the door of our new car.

Stepping out of the car, I had to reach for the ground from the passenger side—the angle was too great from the lean into the water. I walked to the front to see the damage and watched as Nick climbed across the seat to exit from the passenger side—opening the driver's door would have meant flooding the cabin even more.

Looking at the situation I laughed a lot. My phone was pinging, people were sending me messages to see what happened and if we were ok. It was at this point I decided to go back onto Facebook with another live cross and show the outcome.

As I went live comments flooded in, people were desperate to see the car. I laughed when I noticed Nick's son was one of the viewers demanding to see it. I struggled to contain myself as the laughing faces once again streamed up the screen. I flipped the camera and my laughing became hysterics as the stream of laughing emoji continued to flood my screen, almost as much as the flood filled the inside of the car.

Over the course of the next few hours, we tried in vain to dig the car from its bog. We moved logs, we dug, we deflated the tyres, we dug and dug and dug deeper again. Every time we dug down to free the engine from its mud home, it sank a little more, so physically getting under the car was a risk I wasn't too keen to take; but it was a risk I had to take if we were to free it.

To say I was scared would be an accurate assessment; I had a real fear the car would drop onto my head as I tried to clear the mud. I

With my phone pinging with questions to how we were doing, I figured this image best summed up our predicament.

was careful, reaching out with an arm or a longer stick as to not have my head completely under the car. If I was to be pinned I wanted it to be by an arm, but not my head. Nick and I took turns trying to clear the car, but it was all in vain.

When Nick made the call to the taxi, it became apparent we would have to move fast to make their rendezvous. The taxi company had a vehicle close by and the random crossroad we gave was five kilometres from our current location. We had 40 minutes to make it and we were sitting bare foot in the mud.

With feet washed with water from a jerry can, we put shoes on and took off, the final specks of daylight were guiding our path. Making the timing with minutes to spare, we decided to cook some noodles; we figured if we waited to eat, the taxi would be a while and if we cooked them, that typically it would be on time. Sure enough, as soon as we started cooking, a car approached down a road where there would be no others at this time of night. Our taxi hero had arrived.

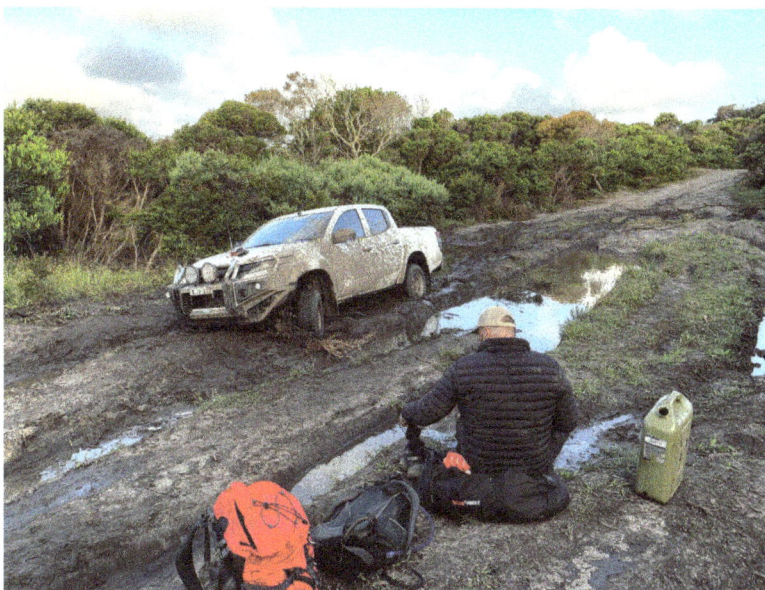

Having made the call, Nick put on his shoes to run to the taxi.
While we knew we'd lost the battle today, we hoped we'd not lose this war.

The taxi driver seemed rightly confused. Here he was, meeting two random guys literally miles from anywhere and covered in mud. The conversation was inquisitive until he came to understand our situation.

The drive along the winding roads took us longer than planned; in the comical nature of this task, the driver inadvertently missed the turn to Apollo Bay, where Nick and I needed to go, but it was an entertaining drive none-the-less. After close to two hours and a $400 taxi fare, we had reached our destination.

The following morning the phone and Facebook were running hot. We had to maintain the comedic relief to our community, so we did a re-cap via yet another Facebook cross. The feedback we received was brilliant! People felt as though they were with us as a part of this adventure, even though many of them were scattered around the country and in some instances the world. The common message was they all wanted to see the vehicle in the light of day.

With recovery gear and the Troopy, we made the two-hour drive back to the car. The scene resembled a battle scene from the World War 1 'Battle of the Somme.' Mud and mud holes scattered all around with trees and branches from our attempts to lever the car now littering the area.

The recovery gear was attached to the Triton, with ramps dug in under the wheels and a strap attaching the Triton to the Troopy. I was in the Troopy ready to drag Nick in the Triton from its muddy resting place. I hit the gas on the Troopy heading forwards, as Nick hit the accelerator with the Triton in reverse.

You could have predicted what was about to happen. We believed the Troopy had the power to mitigate this issue; but, rather than the Troopy pulling the Triton out of the bog, the Triton started pulling the Troopy backwards towards the same muddy fate!

Slamming the brakes on, I launched from the Troopy to detach it from the Triton before we had two cars bogged—that would be the worst-case scenario.

I made the decision to drive an hour, looping back to the other side of the Triton to try pulling it out the other way. While the road on the other side looked worse than the side that we came in on, Nick and I had run it the night prior to meet the taxi, so I at least knew what I was in for. This would be our only hope. Then it happened.

As I turned the key to start the journey, through the vegetation I saw a shadow moving; it was a car coming down the road towards us. The look of horror on the passenger's face contradicted the look of excitement on the drivers. It was married couple, Barry and Jill, who were doing some four-wheel driving of their own.

Now Barry was a madly keen off-road driver and Jill, well it quickly became apparent that she tolerated it. Barry jumped out of the car to see the damage and got right into it. Jill kept saying 'we're not going through that Barry'. It was at this point as Jill was inspecting the damage herself, that Barry came to me and said, 'I have every piece of recovery gear and you have to use it all; Jill doubted I would need any of it when I bought it, so you better use it all'. Laughingly, I agreed.

With that, Barry got his lifting kit from the tray of his ute. I mentioned to him that it would sink into the mud; he didn't care, I was using it. He handed me a ramp to place on the mud as a base plate for the lifter. 'That's two pieces of equipment used in one hit', Barry called to Jill. She stared at him with rolling eyes—she knew what he was doing.

With that failing quickly, Barry had his own snatch strap to be used; even knowing though ours had failed just before their arrival, he was adamant we were to try his. Knowing the fate of this course of action, we played his game and as expected, the Troopy slid back towards the muddy hole. It was at this point that Barry eagerly declared, 'I have a winch! Jill, we're using the winch!' Jill laughed—'that's great Barry, use your winch'.

As the winch was attached to the Triton, the Troopy would be the anchor that tied Barry's ute to the Triton. With all cars hitched together, the task commenced.

I'm in the Troopy acting as an anchor for Barry who is winching Nick from our bog, all under Jill's watchful eye.

As we all radioed to one another we were set, I could feel the weight of Barry's ute pulling at the Troopy. With my foot planted on the brake, Barry pulled the Triton, and I held his car in place. With a shift, I could see the Triton moving for the first time in 24 hours—albeit backwards—but it was moving.

With the Triton finally out of its muddy grave the mood was high, we laughed a lot. I was laughing at Nick, I was laughing at Barry, who was proudly proclaiming to Jill that this one job required every piece of gear she doubted he'd ever use. Nick just looked relieved, but now realised the car had dead flat tyres, and was literally covered and filled with mud. In the chaos of trying to remove the car when we tied it to the Troopy, he had inadvertently forgotten to close the windows and the spinning tyres threw copious amounts of mud into the car; our new car was now filthy, inside and out, not to mention having been filled with water!

If you have ever done any four-wheel driving, you know where I am about to go, if you haven't, well you'll be with Jill.

Barry grabbed his tyre inflation kit, he realised there was one piece of equipment we were yet to use. He proclaimed this to Jill who once again congratulated him as he prepared to pump the tyres on the Triton back to the level they were, literally one day ago. As he did, I decided to go live on Facebook once again.

As I looked at my face staring back at me on the screen, I could see the dirt. We went live and instantly there were at least fifty people waiting to see the damage and to receive an update. Alarmingly and comically, they were all hoping to see us covered in mud and still stuck. That said, there was a lot of excitement that the vehicle was finally out! I interviewed all involved in the extraction of the Triton—the mood was high. Jill was interviewed, she was hilarious, calling us a range of names that seemed to make the audience laugh somewhat even more. As I was wrapping up the interviews, I thanked our community for the fun that this entire situation had afforded us all, closing out the commentary and signing off for the first time with 'that's all from us here, have a great day and remember, at 100%, Adventure lives here'.

THE STANDARD
HAS BEEN SET

You can't really know where you are going until you know where you have been.

Maya Angelou

B orn and raised in a small country town on the south coast of New South Wales, I'm the youngest of five kids. I have two sisters and two brothers. Guy is the eldest and 18 years older than I am. Donna 15 years older, Stephen 13, and Lainie, 5.

If you were to ask my family, they would tell you that I have always had a thirst for some sort of adventure. Now they wouldn't say that I was one of those kids doing crazy things, but I was always in the bush and exploring.

It's funny the things you recall from your childhood. I remember the day I turned three years old—my birthday cake was shaped and decorated as a football. With my Dad at work, I couldn't wait to show it to him, or at least, I was so desperately excited and needed tell him about it now. Mum helped me call him on the phone. I recall his excitement to hear the news of my cake—telling me that he couldn't wait to get home and kick it to me, my screams that he couldn't—it was a cake, he'd smash it.

I sat at the head of the table that night as we lit three candles, I recall the pride I felt on my special day being allowed to sit where dad, as the head of the family normally sat. I can even remember who was sitting where that night.

A year prior to this and I recall the commotion from the people who had the audacity to wake me in the canteen that Mum and Dad were running. Tired, I'd taken myself into the storeroom for a sleep - but nobody knew where I was.

With the ocean only 100 or so metres away; I was blissfully unaware to the fear of my parents and to the teams of people who were searching for me - some of whom had run to the beach to look for me. I remember the look of pure joy on my mother's face when she found me under that chair. Comically, this was possibly the last time I have seen that look of joy; after that day it was looks of curiosity and wonder, (I am laughing at you mum).

As a four-year old, I attended a local preschool. I can still remember the devastating trauma and the feelings of betrayal I held towards my mother as she departed the grounds without me or my knowledge the first day. I recall her telling me we'd 'go and have a look at the preschool' and that we (collectively) 'could play with the other kids'. I recall being intrigued, not wanting to be left there without her.

It's then that I recall the feeling of absolute disloyalty having been excitingly tricked by her to look at the sandpit, her evil ploy to facilitate her escape and leave. Sure, I say this now with a cheeky grin and an internal chuckle, I mean years later I did the same thing to my kids, Abbey, and Drew. It's a great ploy, but it's funny the things you remember and more to the point, how you remember them.

I remember my first day at kindergarten which is the first year of school. I recall my teacher's name (Mrs Moncur). I was in the second of the three classes. I remember how on the first day the teachers got us to run around the oval 'to see who was the fastest'—I guess they needed a break. I remember the name of the kid who was so far in front (Craig) and how the rest of us were all competing for third place, the daylight between Craig and the group was coming in second.

Proudly sitting at the head of the dining table on my third birthday, Lainie next to me with Mum and Stephen.

Life for me as a young kid was 'normal,' I didn't know any different, my family was the same or seemed to be the same as my friends. I had a mum and dad at home, for the most part we ate meat and three vegetables for dinner. We sat at the dinner table in our assigned positions, and I was tormented and tortured daily by Lainie—is that not the role of older and younger siblings? It was normal.

I had a love of sport and adventure and understood the necessary evil of school being there to fill the gaps between play and adventure. I knew school was important, but I was never studious or academic. I did what I had to, I passed my tests, but I was always mentally in the playground or in the bush, I just wanted to be outdoors.

When I was seven years old my parents bought a roller-skating rink—life in this building was to be my new normal.

Mum and Dad now had time and the means to do some amazing things with Lainie and me. The three eldest had all left home by this stage—

Guy had joined the Navy, Donna was married, and Stephen was off working, so at home it was now only four out of the seven of us.

After another few years Mum and Dad decided to open another bakery. They had previously owned a bakery between running the canteen and buying the skating rink. This bakery however was not replacing the skating rink, it was in addition to it—they concurrently ran two separate and vastly different businesses.

It's at this point I started to become more aware of life, I began to see how my family wasn't 'normal' at all, in fact, we were quite odd when you compare our life to the lives that my friends led.

For one, Lainie and I were competitive skaters, representing at a national level. Lainie had been selected to represent Australia, it was

Australian Champion at 8 years old, with Darren Stokes in second and Matthew Pfitzner, third. I was training 13 days on, one day off.

decided that she was too young to compete at a world championships. I had won several Australian titles, but I was coming back into the field as the other kids outgrew my growth. I began to struggle motivationally with our training schedule, which as a 10-year-old was 13 days on and one day off.

Lainie seemed to flourish from my recollection, but she too was starting to change direction. For me, I wanted to play football or soccer with my friends on weekends, this was taking a greater priority for me over being woken at 3am on a Sunday morning to eat soggy weet-bix as we drove to competitions. This was merely one way that I started to become aware that we were anything but 'normal'.

In another example of our family's distance from being anything but a 'normal' household, Lainie and I didn't have our parents at home when we woke for school each day. We would either be already awake or would be woken by mum who called us on the phone at 7am to make sure we were up and that we'd completed our morning training session—10 kilometres on the exercise bike.

By the time we woke each day, Dad had been at work since 2am and Mum with him anywhere from 5 to 6am. Lainie and I made our own breakfast, and we ordered lunch at the 'tuck shop'. The last thing our parents had time for was making lunch, and now I reflect upon it, I don't blame them at all. Not that I did then either, I was a king—I had tuck shop!

Each afternoon dad would collect me from school in his white Honda Civic. We would drive the one kilometre up the hill to the high school to collect Lainie, whose school bell rang at 3:20. I had about 20 minutes of time alone with Dad as we waited for the bell.

I really loved this time with him, we would have all but a few minutes together every day and I loved every one of them—I still think about them. Upon reflecting on this time, I had his full attention and he had mine, I guess this is why I really loved collecting my own kids from school, it was 'our time.'

Lainie and I had a four-hour window with Dad each day and we wanted to make the most of it. I think now about the time I spent playing with my friends after school and just wish I could change it and spend more time with him, just he and I. This is the benefit of hindsight and part of the reason I have shaped my life to be the way it is now.

Even though my family's life and schedule was vastly different to my friends, Lainie and I learnt a lot from Dad. He worked a hell of a lot, and he sacrificed his life for his family, he worked as hard as any man I've met. This is an example of his week.

Each day he would be awake at 1am, be at work no later than 2am, collecting us from school at 3pm; he ate dinner with us as a family around 6pm and was in bed by 7pm. Add to this, there was time to train us for skating, plus he had the maintenance of the house and his relationship with Mum.

On a Friday however, he would not be in bed at 7pm as he was every other night of the work week. On these nights, he would be at the skating rink for the Friday night session which was from 7 until 11pm. He would then clean up and be at home close to midnight—the man was awake for 23 hours each Friday! On Saturday, he'd be up at 7am to be back at the skating rink by 8am to have a 9am to noon session, a 2 to 5pm session and another from 7 to 11pm.

Sunday was a sleep in for him. He had a Sunday afternoon session at the rink which was from 2 to 5pm after which he would clean up once again, be at home for dinner around 6pm and back in bed at 7pm, only to be back at the bakery not later than 2am the following morning and start all over again. Add to this, when it was competition season, he would be waking us at 3am on Sunday mornings to drive to Sydney for us to race, this was his routine.

One thing that Mum and Dad taught me was that when you work for someone, you need to provide your boss with three to five times the value for what they're paying you—that is, to make your employment worth their while. This is something that has stuck with me my entire life.

When you think about the hours worked, you can see the value my parents placed on an employee. You can imagine how fast they would have employed someone they could trust to work independently and without supervision—that person would've been invaluable.

Strive to be that person was their guidance to me, stating that when I achieved this standard, I would find myself employed for life. It's something I've be driven to provide those who've employed me, and it's something that now as a business owner I strive to find in potential employees.

The hardest lesson is something I learned quickly with my own business—that is, nobody will invest physically and emotionally into your business the way that you do; they may believe in your brand, but not like you! The culture of the brand is the thing I strive to foster. A person emotionally invested in your brand is as close as you will get to your level of dedication and commitment.

The one thing that we have all been driven for and I think I have had the chance to do this more than my parents, mainly as my business is more inclusive with participation—is making people believe in your product. I believe it's far easier to achieve when you sell bucket list adventure holidays rather than cakes and roller skating. That said, both Mum and Dad did it well, and I would hate to compete with them on a comparable playing field.

The one thing that all kids in my family can agree on is that we were all subjected to Dad's favourite quote. To this day we all cringe when one of us says it at a family gathering—'don't tell me what you're going to do, tell me what you've done'. Dad loved this quote—we all hated it. It would be said to us every time one of us had a grand life plan, or even something we wanted to do that day. Noting there were five kids, you can imagine!

Dad's constant point was that there are many people in the world with hopes, dreams, and aspirations, and only a few have a road map of how they'll succeed. Dad wanted us to be people of action, not discussion and this was his way of saying the same thing that Mum would say to me years later, albeit in a very different way, 'Don't wait for your ship to dock, swim to it', or as Kurt Cobain once said, 'if opportunity doesn't knock, build a door'. While all said differently they're the same message. People don't give you things, you have to make your own opportunities, so go and take what you want and don't wait for a free ride or a handout. Dad's way was just really irritating, which is part of the reason why he loved it so much.

COMMENCING THE ADVENTURE JOURNEY

'The problem I have with Cameron is that he has literally no idea what he wants to do with his life'.

My high school career guidance counsellor.

What did you want to be when you grew up? Did you know? If you knew, did it come to fruition?

It was hard for my dream job to become a reality, career-wise I had no idea what I wanted to do with my life. I remember my kindergarten teacher asking us to draw a picture of what we wanted to be when we grew up. I drew a ship with a stick figure on it, saying I wanted to be in the Navy.

Why the Navy? Well both Dad and Guy served in the Navy, and I grew up in a town where there was a large naval presence, so this is what I thought I knew. I didn't know the first thing about being in the Navy other than you went on ships, my dad had worked on helicopters—and you were away from home a lot. If I had been asked to detail the roles within the Navy, even asked what my father and brother did, I didn't really know.

I literally had no real knowledge of any profession other than the jobs my family had. I knew some people built things, I knew they worked on job sites, in shops and in offices, but I didn't know what they actually did, I'd never thought about it. I'd seen people on the roads surveying, and I was always intrigued, but I held no aspirations to actually do it. I had zero clue.

I think back to my childhood and find it almost fate that things ended up the way they did, I didn't shape it this way, it just seemed to happen. One minute I was at school in Sydney, the next thing I was living back on the coast playing a high level of representative rugby, harbouring a desire to make a career in the pre-professional period of the sport. Not knowing what I wanted to do, I'd like to think I was smart by not commencing a university degree. There was a good chance that I wouldn't have been inspired to study for it, let alone enjoyed it, or ever used the training—to me that was a waste of time and money.

I looked at the local Technical College, I wanted to see the courses they had on offer. While there were many, there was only one that resonated with me—it was a carpentry pre-apprenticeship. The successful completion of this course would take one year off an actual apprenticeship and take two years off the academic requirement; it meant upon the completion of this course that I was an attractive option to a potential employer in the construction industry.

I enjoyed the course, and I really enjoyed the content. In my spare time I was working with a building company that specialised in steel frames. While the pay was good, I hated working for this dysfunctional company. This had me starting to question if I wanted to be in this line of work at all.

It was during this year that I received my second offer to play rugby for a high-profile club in Sydney, they were however unable to assist me with employment other than picking up glasses in a local club. With the news that I was in contact with this club and a move back to Sydney pending, the country club I had been playing for found me an apprenticeship as an electrician with one of our lower grade players, a man called Col Williams.

I knew Col well enough to say hello to him, but that was about it. Col was happy to pursue this agreement, but wanted to see my resume first, so I took it to him late one night (I don't know why) and like all 18-year-olds, it was filled with a heap of crap. It was an impressive document for someone who had never worked full-time—let's say that much.

Col agreed that I would start but noted that as I had snapped my collarbone in the game the weekend prior, I'd start my apprenticeship in two weeks' time, when my collarbone was a little better.

The catalyst for the decision for me to pursue this line of work was more than just rugby, it was after a conversation I'd had with Dad.

Dad had just built a room in our house. In order to make one large room two smaller rooms, dad installed a wall, plastered and painted it, but he had to ask a friend who was an electrician to come and do the electrical work.

In this conversation, Dad had said, 'any idiot like me can build a room or a house, but you actually need an electrician to wire it, I think you need to choose a career where people need you more'. He was right, Dad had years prior built a house, but he needed someone to wire it. With the offering of a job with greater prospects, I chose to stay, play Rugby in the country and become an electrician.

The first day of my apprenticeship was my final day wearing a sling for my collarbone. I arrived early, I had a coffee with Col and his wife, Tracy, and we headed off to start my career as an electrician.

My first job in the trades was to push start his old van, something that I would do each morning for two years. As we drove off Col laid the ground rules, 'Right, don't lie to me, if you want to go drinking with your mates and play golf, tell me, I'll probably come too, but don't lie to have a day off. Don't fail college. I will pay for you to go the first time, but I will not pay for you to go back. If you fail, that's on you—got it?' Got it! Easy! I can do that I said, he looked back to the road, and we drove on, that was that.

One minute later his head snapped to the left. He looked at me with a horrified look, asking with an alarmed tone 'you're not colour blind, are you?' 'No' I laughed at him. His demeanour eased, 'ah! Good', then followed up with 'don't mess with the red one, that one bites!' Noted, I said while nodding.

I had an amazing time working with Col, I learnt a lot—about a lot of things. Col was never the snappiest dresser, so at times, first impressions were hit and miss from people—but when he spoke, and through his actions that first impression changed very quickly.

Col was intelligent, very intelligent and had a lot of street smarts—he had been around the block a few times. I recall one occasion a man called him a short, fat, bald, pommy (c-word). Col's reply was on point, teaching me that getting upset doesn't solve anything and that agreeing with them shoots down their insult pretty fast. Col replied 'Short—yep, fat—agreed, bald—hard to argue, pommy—yes I am, (c-word), oh come on mate, that's a little steep, I'd say I'm a prick, what's your point?' the guy had no re-call. I loved it!

Col and I had a ball together and became great mates. I completely trust him, and would like to think that he trusts me too, but he has the ability to never forget something that you did incorrectly or broke. He would regale to this day a story of something that I broke in 1994—the man is a sponge!

Did I love being an electrician? Not one bit, but I didn't hate it either. What I loved most about being an electrician was the people I worked with; I loved working with them, they were so much fun. We worked hard, man we worked hard, but we had so many laughs along the way. I am eternally grateful to Col and later his business partner Wayne and their wives for the lessons they taught me in this really critical and formative time of my life. Together, they afforded me the chance to live, fail and learn in a safe environment. I owe them so much.

Upon the completion of my apprenticeship, I was ready to explore as much of the world as I could. I had lived, partied and worked hard for the previous five years, I was at the point where I needed to explore so much more than the small town where I lived. While I loved where I was from, I knew there was a big world out there and I didn't want to be one of the people who never left. I always believed that if I returned, I would know that I'd had other experiences in my life. Together with my girlfriend Margie, we moved to Queensland. We both loved it there, so it seemed like a cool place to live for a bit before I decided what to do next.

This was where the same problem reared its ugly head once again—what would I do with my life?

While I had enjoyed being an electrician, and I was pretty good at it too, being named the Apprentice of the Year in my final year, I didn't launch out of bed every day to go and pull cables. It was and would always remain a means to an end for me, I was never inspired to think about it more than I had to. I wanted more for my life, but what that was, I remained unsure.

I started doing odd jobs around the place. I mowed lawns, I did yards, I worked as a handyman for a few estate agents on their property management teams, and I also did some electrical work. The thing I learned in Queensland was there are so many people willing to take advantage of a tradesman; I had to stop being nice to people, they were just taking me for a ride. I found I started to get short with people and refused to back down. This wasn't me, it's not what I wanted to be like and not how I wanted to spend my life.

It was during my time in Queensland that Dad happened to get work close by, working on a defence contract at a nearby Army base. Not being able to find suitable staff to fill many of the roles, Dad asked me to run the base gym for him. With my agreeance, he flippantly said 'you never know, you may want to join the Army one day'. I laughed at him with the reply of 'good on you'—to me the thought was ridiculous.

Having started this role however, I saw the Army for the first time, I was somewhat captivated by it all and the thought of Dad's comment started running through my head over and over again. I began to wonder if this had all worked out for some crazy reason I didn't yet understand or appreciate. I am usually pretty perceptive with life, but I started questioning myself—what had I missed?

SIMPLE CHOICES MADE DIFFICULT

Your life is a result of your choices. If you don't like your life, it's time to make better choices.

Zig Ziglar

Let me ask you a question to ponder. Have you ever walked into a restaurant knowing exactly what you wanted? If you have, did you take a menu and if you did, why did you take it? You knew what you wanted before you walked through the door.

I bet for many of you who faced this predicament there's a good chance you changed your mind when faced with choice. You knew what you wanted when you walked in, but it's fair to assume you over-complicated a simple decision when faced with many suitable choices.

If you're like me, you looked at what the other patrons were eating, and you looked at the other menu items being served, you started to see other options so vastly different to what you wanted. There's a fair chance you ended up with something so far removed from your initial intention. This was me with career choices.

The difference with my career however, was that I was yet to realise what it was that I wanted for my metaphorical dinner. I see now that I was always meant to be in the Army; I had just never considered it.

Towards the completion of my schooling, I contemplated the Navy, and was unsuccessful in an application for the Australian Defence Force Academy. I had never even considered the Army, that is until I saw it for myself at 24-years of age. It was then I finally knew what I was meant to do with my life.

In order for me to explain how I knew this was my destiny, I once again have to go back in time.

I would have been 10 or 11 years old when the movie *Rambo, First blood, part II* was released. My friends and I watched it over and over again—we loved it! Inspired, every afternoon after school and on weekends, we'd head into the bush to play 'Rambo'. We'd stalk one another trying to find where the others were hiding, we'd make booby traps to defeat each other, trying to hunt out the others, all having the same idea—we all wanted to be Rambo.

I think about my mate Jeff, who was so into it, he made his mum buy him camouflage pants and the 'Rambo knife', the knife which had a compass, wire cutters, and waterproof matches all stored in the handle—he was the coolest! We all had a knife for fighting; I mean we were 11-years old, who didn't need a knife for fighting? While we all wanted to be Rambo, if we couldn't, we'd all settle for being Jeff with the pants and the knife.

I became aware much later in life when I joined the Army that I don't ever recall being lost in the bush; I seemed to always have the awareness of my direction and where I was at all times. I knew where north was, I could tell direction using the sun and stars and I seemed to be able to find my mates somewhat faster than they could me. I could sense the disturbance to the ground where they'd placed their booby traps and I knew what to look for through the foliage to see what was different in appearance—be it a shine, a shape, a shadow or a surface.

How is it that I never saw I was suited to this life and the potential to have this career earlier? Who knows! What I do know is that I get chronically seasick and the only cure for seasickness is the shade from a tree. Why did I think about the Navy and not the Army? If you can answer that one, where the hell were you when I was 17!

What I know is that as soon as I became exposed to life in the Army, I knew I wanted more. As I mentioned, I never thought about electrical work when I wasn't actually at work, but here I was, still yet to join the Army and it was all I could think about. I shared a house with a guy called Troy, he was in the Army. I bled him for information day and night—I must have been a menace. I studied it—we watched war movies together, we'd discuss the tactics being used in the movie. I even remember being at the casino on the Gold Coast where he and his mates taught me 'target indications' using the bar, poker machines and a big screen as target reference points. I was taught 'fire control orders' as drink orders, 'two beers and a rum' being like callsign 1A, 20 rounds rapid, callsign 1B, ghosting—fire! I could picture it, I understood it, I loved it—that was it! I was joining the Army.

I made an appointment at the local recruiting office on the Gold Coast to talk about joining. They showed me some videos and arranged an appointment for me to go to the main recruiting office in Brisbane.

Passing the threshold into the recruiting office in Brisbane I heard a familiar voice call out to me—it was a mate from the Army base—Rob.

Rob is a brilliant guy, I love him, and he was as excited to see me as I was him. Rob was thrilled that I wanted to join, recommending I complete the entry test. Rob informed me that by undertaking this test, the Army could assess my aptitude, this would detail which roles I was allowed to apply for.

The test was easy enough with speed responses to questions such as toe is to foot as finger is to? A—chair, B—dog, C—hand, D—Car. Sure, there were far harder questions than this, but you get the point. I also completed a mathematics version of this same test with basic calculations—like addition, subtraction, division, and multiplication, but some far harder equations too. Having been an electrician, maths was my thing.

There were some hard questions, but on the whole, it seemed reasonably fine. When I finished, I knew I hadn't shown I was awaiting my inclusion into Mensa, but I knew I'd displayed I was educated with a basic understanding of english and mathematics. I waited for the results.

Rob walked back to see me and asked me a very simple question, 'do you want a career or a job?' I'd never really considered this, 'a car-reer?' I replied in a long and inquisitive tone, almost waiting for him to answer what I thought to be his own rhetorical question.

I figured that at 24 years of age, maybe it was time to look forward with a little more longevity than I had previously. Rob advised me that I had passed the test well enough to apply for the Royal Military College (RMC) in the suburb of Duntroon, Canberra. The Royal Military College is where Army Officers are trained for their first appointments in the Australian Army. I thought about it for a little while and with Rob's guidance decided I would apply for Duntroon. In the event that I was unsuccessful with this application, I would join as a soldier—no matter what happened, I would be joining the Army.

The application process for selection to Duntroon was long! I did a further day of testing where I completed a psychological assessment, wrote two separate essays, one on why I wanted to be in the Army and the second on why I wanted to be an officer, not a soldier. I did another more substantial aptitude test, plus interviews with both a psychologist and a recruiting officer, who was a Captain in the Army.

It was recommended that my application proceed to the next stage of the process, the Army Officer Selection Board. This is what I would later describe as 'the mentally taxing day from hell'.

This was a 12-hour day, where with the other candidates, I underwent a series of tests, interviews, panels, and activities. We were all competing to be selected for one of the few positions on offer. This process has been used to select officers since World War 2, and it's a day that you never forget.

While I recall the entire day with clarity, the most interesting part for me was the interviews. I was the fifth to be interviewed. The interviews prior to mine were so long that I watched an entire movie in the waiting room before my turn—my interview went for no more than five minutes.

The room was muggy, a ceiling fan circling above one of the selection team, an Engineering Officer, Major Murray. I looked at the board—sitting in the middle was the board president, to the left of him, Major Murray, to the right was a psychology Major whom I'd met previously at recruiting.

The board president began; he smiled briefly and asked how I was. I replied with a smile, 'I am well thank you sir'. He asked how I had found the day so far, I paused, considered and replied, 'it's been challenging, I've spent the day trying to remain like a good apprentice should, which is trying to stay one step ahead of my master, trying to think forward and that while I've been mildly stressed because I know how much I want this, I've actually really enjoyed the process'. He smiled and without hesitation stated that he knew that I had played representative rugby for New South Wales Country in the under 21's, highlighting that Duntroon had been beaten by the Defence Academy that year, asking me what I thought of that. I must have looked strangely at him, because I felt it an odd question in this forum, but replied, 'I would like to be a part of fixing that problem next year, sir'. He seemed somewhat satisfied with that response and smiled. He turned to Major Murray, asking him if he had any questions for me—he had one.

Major Murray was a quietly spoken man and when he asked his question the ceiling fan immediately above him muffled his soft voice. I saw his mouth move, but I didn't hear what he'd asked. I spoke up and said, 'you'll have to excuse me sir, I couldn't hear you over the fan'. He repeated his question, louder this time so as I could hear him—'I said, do you think you could look through the optic sight of a weapon and pull the trigger, killing another human?'

I paused and considered my reply. This answer would tell the board how I thought. It was an unprovoked question seeking a spontaneous reply—impossible to plan for. I knew that if I were to answer yes, I might appear a psychopath, fool hardy, or both. If I said no, then I may not be fit to join the Army, let alone possess the ability to lead people as an officer into dangerous situations.

I paused for no longer than three seconds and said, 'Sir, I don't know, I have never been in a position like that to know either way. But what I do know, is that if I am selected for the Army and I find myself in that position, there is going to be a strategic, operational and a tactical requirement for me to do so, I will have been trained to do it, so I would like to think that yes I could'. He remained emotionless and said that he had no more questions. The president looked to his left and asked the psychologist if she had any questions; she replied that she'd interviewed me at recruiting, she had no questions.

I was thanked and asked to send forward the next candidate. As I walked back into the waiting room, I saw the opening credits of the next movie. The others asked me what had happened, I explained that I'd been interviewed: I think we all wondered if I had crashed and burned. I realise now that I'd already given them enough that day, the interview was merely a formality.

I received a letter advising me that I had been successful at the board and that I would progress to the next phase of the selection process. In this phase, all successful applicants from across the country are compared, rated, and ranked from best to worst. This was personally the toughest part of the entire process as it was completely out of my hands.

Once it has been decided how many places will be offered for the following intake to Duntroon, the ranking list of candidates is used, and places offered to those people within the allocated number. I was advised that there would be 84 places on offer to commence training in January 2000.

I'd not heard anything for weeks and I was growing impatient. I called Rob to see if he was able to find anything out for me. He calmed me down and told me that he would do what he could, but this waiting period was quite normal for this process.

Two days later Rob called, instantly I could tell he was excited. 'Congratulations sir, you are going to RMC. Letters are being sent out this week to make you an offer'. I was over the moon. Rob told me that I had smashed the selection board and that in all of Australia, I was ranked second.

While ecstatic, I was also aware that sometimes you have to be careful what you wish for.

It was time for me to have a career, not a job.
The Army was always my destiny, just nobody told me, and I hadn't realised either.
Standing with Dad at the Royal Military College, Duntroon having completed the basic
training phase, the first six-weeks of 18 months.

BEING INCULCATED WITH A SET OF VALUES

The aim of military training is not just to prepare men for battle, but to make them long for it.

Louis Simpson

On 27 January 2000 I woke from a broken sleep; today was the day that would change my life forever. I dressed into my suit, collected my bags and was driven by Margie to the Defence Force Recruiting office in Brisbane. Today I was to be sworn into the Australian Defence Force.

It was a morning of mixed emotions. When would I next see Margie? What would the following weeks look like? What would happen? Was it like in the movies with the screaming and yelling? What would I endure? I just didn't know. One thing I knew, was that I was embarrassed—one of the items we had to take was an ironing board. Here I was, walking down the street in a suit and tie, a bag over my shoulder, and a bloody ironing board under my arm like some kind of poor man's surfboard. Wait! When would I surf again? I hadn't even considered that until literally right now.

Having been sworn into the Army, I stood with the others waiting to board the bus. I recall a woman who worked at the recruiting office was not too happy about us standing around. She started yelling at us to move and when we didn't move fast enough for her liking, she yelled that when we got to Kapooka (where soldiers are trained) the Corporals would 'sort us out'.

One of the guys laughed at her, telling her that we were going to RMC, not Kapooka; she muttered something and stormed off. I saw this as the last minor victory we would have for a while.

Having boarded the bus, with my bags and ironing board underneath, a shallow 'what have I done' feeling came over me. I looked out the window to Margie who was waving and giving me a 'call me when you can' hand signal. With a blown kiss and a look of sadness, the bus pulled away. I was now in the Army and leaving her for what would be the first of many times.

Upon our arrival at Brisbane Airport, if I was embarrassed about walking with the ironing board through the city earlier, it was about to be quadrupled. We walked as one group, like when well-dressed sporting teams walk through an airport, but with heckles from passers-by such as 'ah the Australian ironing team' and laughter aimed at us. One thing for sure, I was glad to get that thing checked in. We took our places and departed, bound for Canberra.

I will always remember the fear that struck me when I saw Brenton Pearse and Jack Egan for the first time. These men stood inside the Canberra Airport in a uniform I now know to be 'Poly's Ceremonial'. With uniforms starched, creases lifting into the sky as one, 'Blues Caps' and carrying what people in defence know to be a 'Pace Stick'; these are carried by a Regimental Sergeant Major and by Drill Sergeants at the Royal Military College. I looked at these men and thought that I was going to stay as far away from them as I could, they looked angry and as scary as hell.

One of the guys from my plane with bag and ironing board in hand walked up to them and said, 'excuse me Sergeant' and before he could utter another word, he was informed in the most direct manner known to man to shut up, get his personal belongings under the bus and him onto it as quickly as he could. I just walked to the bus without talking to them, thinking all the while to stay the hell away from those two blokes.

The bus ride to RMC takes no more than ten minutes and it was the quietest ten minutes of my life. There were about twenty people on board.

We arrived at the college and as I stepped off the bus, I looked up at the old white buildings and thought, 'here we go'. We were gathered near a set of stairs and another man dressed like the other two scary blokes at the airport said in what appeared to be a much more pleasant manner, 'When you hear your name, say Sergeant, grab your things and wait over there', pointing to an area off to the side. Campbell—Sergeant, Cuerel—Sergeant, Gordon—Sergeant, James—Sergeant—I didn't need to hear another name, I got my things and walked over to be met with the next person that was called. I met him on the plane, Joel—another guy from Queensland. We were walked up the hill to a barracks building; I asked the cadet leading us where we were headed, 'Gallipoli Company' was all he replied, and I wasn't asking any more.

Walking into the company there were people everywhere; it resembled a friendlier version of what Dad had told me about his first day in the Navy when people tried to bash him. I wondered how it had been for him all those years ago—I didn't want to think about it for one second longer. I was scared enough having heard his stories, and here I was eight years older than he was when he did this. I was scared and apprehensive enough to consider the fights starting. That said, I think that would have helped, it would have let some of my anxiety out; it was the fear of the unknown that I learned to hate.

Allocated a room, I was told to put on 'PT clothes' (sports clothes) and to be in the foyer in two minutes. What! Two minutes, I was now in what they call the 'shock of capture phase'.

Formed up and marched for the first time, we were led to a storeroom where they issue clothing—for now it would be only a shiny material navy-blue tracksuit, the RMC badge on the left of the jacket. Navy-blue sports shorts with a red stripe were issued to wear beneath the track suit, as were plain white socks. Gallipoli Company were given light blue T-Shirts—this was our uniform for the next few days. We were led back to the company and given a stencil and a black marker, we were instructed to write our surnames on the front, a direct line from armpit to armpit and written above that imaginary line, not below it. My name 'James' written across

my new light blue shirt—I was officially now known by rank and title—
Staff Cadet James.

As I stood in my room that night well and truly in the shock of capture—I
wondered what I had done, why had I wanted this, what was I going to do? I
thought of Dad, I thought of Margie, I wondered what she was doing right
now, I wished I was there with her. I remembered the last time that I had
been in Canberra, it was a great trip and here I was now standing in a room
at Duntroon, listening to the unfamiliar noises outside my door. I looked
at the lights towards the airport, seeing a plane taking off and just wishing I
was on it—I didn't care where it was going—I just wanted to be anywhere but
here at this moment.

I remembered the call I made to Mum on the third night from boarding
school. I was in tears and wanting her to come and get me, homesickness for
the first time had set in. I remembered the feelings of missing my comforts
of home, and I also remember my mother holding tough on the phone,
telling me that she wasn't coming to get me, I had to do the term—ten weeks.
If I still felt the same way after one school term, she'd remove me without
question.

I remembered the feeling I had that night was comparable to this one I
had right now, nothing was different, and nothing would change. I thought
I just had to take each day and not to wish away an opportunity; get through
the first few days and it will all be ok. Self-doubt crept in no matter how much
positivity I tried convincing myself with. I lay in my new bed trying to sleep,
tomorrow is the first day of I don't know what—thinking and reflecting as I
lay there on what I had learned in that first week at boarding school—tough
times never last, tough people do I would tell myself over and over, and that's
when the yelling started.

With my sheets over my shoulder, standing to attention in the hallway,
thinking to myself, when in doubt, dominate, when in doubt, dominate—
you got this, this was my new reality and this mantra kept running through
my head over and over.

While being at RMC had its moments, it was a lot of fun. I will always remember the fun and the horrific times. I remember in my initial phase of training being in the bush and being taught to navigate. We would do it as a member of a team of 10 people, then in smaller groups of four and then we were sent to do it by ourselves, at first only in the daytime and later by both day and night. It was at these times I remembered being a kid in the bush and would smile to myself. I loved the thought of what being in the Army offered me and what I offered it.

Don't let the black eye fool you, it was from a rugby game. For a sport that gave me so much joy and opportunity, it was now on the cusp of taking so much away. I wouldn't let it ruin my career in the Army.

I loved the navigation exercises. You were all alone in the bush and you weren't being yelled at or treated like an idiot. Don't get me wrong, while I hated it then, I agree with it now that I understand why they do it, but at the time, the solace I took from my own personal space was meditative.

It was on these days when I would think back to being a kid all alone in the bush. I loved it and loved the experience of being there with my army uniform on, remembering Jeff and wondering if he'd be jealous that I now not only had the pants, but the entire ensemble—plus! Who needed the Rambo knife—I had a rifle and a bayonet.

Much of the time at the college we were busy being busy. We were taught a lot about a wide range of topics, such as the tactics of fighting both offensively and defensively. We were also stuffed around a lot too. Why? Because they could—well that was my belief. That said, I formed my own opinion that we were being deliberately stuffed around to know what it felt like, that is, so we never did it to the soldiers. To be fair, I think that 98% of us would have taken this away from these instances, but I think there would have been at least one to two percent that would think this is how you treat people. To me, it was an implied lesson that didn't really need to be taught.

We had exercises where we rarely slept, we were tired, hungry and in the most of extreme environmental conditions. As an example, in the second of three six-month blocks we had an exercise which was based around food and sleep deprivation. On the surface this seems pretty straight forward—don't feed them or let them sleep. The reality of this was there was an entire scenario which started a week prior—a week of 'pre-fatigue'. We attended compulsory sports on the Saturday and were expected to 'muster' at the college at 8pm that night. While we had a fair idea what was about to occur, noting we'd been flogged all week with little rest, it was at this muster it became apparent that the food and sleep deprivation exercise was about to start, we'd been expecting it—it was upon us.

Individually we were given a one-day ration pack and told that we'd be issued more. My mate Meds and I were quick to see through this, we knew if this was the exercise we'd been expecting and we knew it was, we knew there would be no more food on offer.

We'd been led to the gym where we filled out papers and more papers and even more papers, papers that kept 'getting lost', so time and again we would fill these out, all an attempt to keep us awake for as long as possible.

At approximately 4am we were driven to a nearby training area where we were finally allowed to sleep—we were exhausted. We would have slept at best for not more than 15 minutes when there was a massive explosion in the shed were we slept, a team of terrorists burst through the door—we'd been taken hostage.

Having been taken hostage, or 'prisoners-of-war' we were tied together and made to sit in lines of ten. We were yelled at for hours and made to stand up when they hit a bin with a stick and then to sit down when they hit it again. For hours at a time, we would do this until they would pass us onto someone else to physically destroy us, that is until we were either passed out on the ground and or being physically sick from exhaustion.

It was during this time we were questioned in a 'resistance to interrogation' style. I remember being forced to sit in a building with my team, our heads covered with black hoods. We'd been in there for a while when one of the terrorists burst through the door and asked for the person in charge. Standing up was never a thought in my mind, for one, I wasn't the one in charge, but even if I was, it was never going to happen. Now it was at this point that although I couldn't see what happened, with my head covered by the hood, I felt it and I heard it, the guy next to me, who was in charge stood up, much to the comic relief of the terrorists and much to our disdain. I couldn't believe he was so dumb, to me this was lesson 101, humanise yourself, but don't make out you're someone important within the group.

I am guessing here as I had no concept of time, it could have been an hour or it could have been two minutes, but around ten minutes later the terrorist burst back in the door asking for the second-in-command, followed by 'and before you want to play stupid games, we know it's you Mr Cuerel; Mr Campbell being your section commander has you all detailed by position in his notebook'. With that, Cuerel stood up and I am guessing was led away.

When it came my turn to be interrogated, I was very well aware that this was a training exercise, and that I wouldn't be harmed—that was the logical side of my brain. Then there's the illogical side of your brain that starts screaming at you, especially when your head is in a hood, you can't see your captor and a pistol barrel drives into the side of your skull and is cocked—you start to think 'maybe the Army was a bad choice after all'.

Two days of this and we were physically spent. Having been in minor stress positions for hours at a time and awake for close to three days, we were at breaking point. Then the exercise took a turn in that we were 'freed', but our belongings were spread over kilometres of bushland—our first job was to find it all. We were informed however, that if the 'enemy' found us, they were able to take our one-day ration pack, and we would not be given more. What I took away from all of this was that I would be in the bush for at least a week, there was a good chance it was going to snow, it was unlikely that I would sleep, and I wouldn't be fed.

While this exercise sounds horrific—and in parts it was—I don't recall ever laughing as much as I did that week. It proved me right with knowing who I could and couldn't rely on.

We started with over ten people in our section and finished with five; that's five people doing the same amount of work, the same amount of lifting and carrying the same amount of equipment that ten should. We managed to get by just fine—actually we did better than fine. We had a tight knit team that not only trusted one another, but relied on one another—is that not the perfect example of a team?

I remember so many things about that week, even though we were dog tired. If you were to ask, Meds, he would laugh to this day if you were to do a 'landmine' hand signal, he would likely yell at you 'It's not a minefield, it's a mountain bike track!' If you were to ask him where Cuerel was, he would tell you that Cuerel was asleep two kilometres away sitting bolt upright in the middle of the road. If you were to ask him about 'anxiety' he would tell you about another mate, Jeff, who 'died a notional death' for removing his chemical mask and us having to dig his grave, which we ended up making him dig himself. If you were to ask him to comment about walking barefoot through the position during the rare opportunity we had ten minutes to sleep, he would tell you that it was him, not me, pissing against a tree and shrugging when questioned if he thought it the right thing to be doing. I got into a lot of trouble for that one, I still laugh about it.

It was a week of comical events that we remember with clarity to this day. I loved it!

Life at the college was a mix of emotions. I remember feeling constantly anxious. The more anxious I was, the more anxious I became—I was anxious about my anxiety! It was a constant cycle of emotions for me. I began to stress out about my anxiety, but I couldn't put my finger on the cause. I didn't call it anxiety; all I knew was that I couldn't slow my mind from a million racing thoughts at once, these thoughts were in no logical order.

Upon reflection, I can tell you exactly what it was and when it started. The thing with Duntroon is that it's meant to showcase your abilities

My first exposure to Armoured Personnel Carriers, at the Puckapunyal Army Base in Victoria.
Little did I know at this point, but I would spend many years 'mechanised' in these vehicles, I loved them! I did not however love the cold weather this day.

and increase your confidence. For me, being a little older than most, joining at 24, and being a licensed electrician, I was a confident young man. Getting more confident would have had me appear arrogant, which was the last thing I wanted, so the only real way for my confidence to go, was down.

It was in the first of three six-month blocks when it happened. Life for me was moving along well, when in a routine game of rugby for the college, I was tackled slightly from the side—my knee exploded. I knew that I was badly hurt with some major damage; the pain was immense. The swelling was almost instantaneous.

Noting how badly I wanted this as a career, I had been at the college long enough to know the attitude towards those who broke and those who appeared inadequate. With this injury I was now firmly in both groups. Sure, upon reflection, this couldn't have been further from the truth, but at that time this was my reality.

It was during my rehabilitation for a ruptured posterior cruciate ligament that the remainder of the college went on a two-week training exercise into the bush.

Unable to attend with my injury, I found myself with the other broken trainees from all classes within the college, some had been in the Army for as long as four years—I was in my fifth month. I was in a very small group and many eyes assessing our attitude and our ability.

During this time, we were assessed on our ability to deliver command orders. It was to be my first encounter of others setting out to make themselves look better at your expense—an attitude that was rife in the college. I recall giving a set of orders; it was like watching wolves on their prey as the more senior and experience trainees started to pull apart piece by piece my verbal presentation, all to make themselves look more impressive. It was something I would begin to notice a lot more as the months wore on.

Added to this and the pressure of not wanting to look silly, was the very real prospect that should I not recover fast enough, I would have to do another six months of training, or worse still—be discharged as medically unfit for service. This would be my worst case scenario, something I'd already witnessed a lot, and something I desperately wanted to avoid: so I trained hard with my rehabilitation.

I trained at least three times a day and I did more than I was being asked to do. I was leaving nothing to chance.

When the remainder of the college returned, I was given a formal warning for having failed to attend the training exercise. While a formality, I was happy that the officer giving me the warning spoke highly of me, but he cautioned, if I failed to attend the following two exercises, I would likely be medically removed from training—all for a game of rugby. A game that had given me so much, like an apprenticeship, and other opportunities, was now on the cusp of taking so much away from me.

While the remainder of the college went on a mid-semester holiday—I went into the bush on a training exercise. I had to catch up on what I had missed. While my friends were at the beach and having fun, myself and the others who'd missed the last exercise would all be in the wet negative seven-degree temperatures of a Canberra winter, trying to keep our Army dreams alive. It was a hard week and one that I reflect upon a lot. Why? This is why.

I have always said to my kids that the fastest way from Sydney to Brisbane is via the highway. It's fast, efficient and you tend not to learn too much. If you were to take the country and the coastal roads, you pass through a lot of small towns. It takes a lot longer; you stop more, and you see and learn more. My Duntroon 'drive' was now on a minor detour, a detour where I wanted only one additional stop, not a route change.

With this exercise behind me, I was back on track. I trained hard and was seen to be doing the right thing. Leading into graduation, and with the culmination of 18 months of hard work now only days away, I had a bad feeling I may still be medically downgraded because of the injury. Being medically downgraded would mean I was ineligible to graduate—I walked into the medical centre and asked if I was downgraded, to both their and my alarm, I was!

In order to graduate I had to have the highest medical classification; I was on the third level! With an alarmed tone the nurse asked, 'you haven't been on any exercises, have you?' and my reply, 'ah yeah, all of them!' She ran in to see the doctor. He asked me to come into his office. He asked what had happened to my knee, when it had happened, and when I went back into the bush. Most importantly to him, he wanted to know why I went back into the bush without being medically cleared to do so. He grabbed my file and started to read through it.

I explained how I was never informed I had to be raised in classification to go back into the bush, this was an oversight of mine and highlighted my lack of understanding on the system. I explained that I had been cautioned on my warning not to miss another exercise, if I did, I risked going back in training and or being medically discharged, so when I felt I was strong enough, I got back to work.

He thoroughly assessed my knee, completing stability tests, including folding it, bending it and hitting it with the reflex hammer, no issues. He then pinched the edges of the kneecap, I yelped, he laughed, saying at least he could get one reaction from me. Chuckling he said that I'd clearly worked hard on my rehabilitation and that I must clearly want this career, grabbing his pen and changing me back to the highest classification—a process that usually requires a review board. He was happy with my knee, he was happy with me, and I was happy, I was back on track to graduate with my peers.

When the day came for me to graduate, Margie, who was now my wife of six months, asked me if I was happy about graduating. My reply was honest, accurate, and not the answer she'd hoped or thought she'd get. 'Happiest day of my life' I replied, yes, even more than our wedding day. Margie was horrified—I explained.

Every day with her was a great day, whereas every day at the college was a painstaking challenge where I was treated like crap. With my graduation and being treated that way now over, I was just so happy—being with her hadn't changed. She said she understood but did she really; I still smile writing this thinking that she thought I was a cold-hearted prick about it. I could and should have just said 'yes, I am happy'.

The day after graduating, I was asked to go and see my Drill Sergeant, Jack Egan. That's right, he was one of the men I was terrified of at the airport just 18 months prior. For the past six months, Sergeant Egan (Jack) and I had held weekly meetings to talk life, the college, and other related issues. On each occasion he'd ask me if I wanted a brew (a coffee)—he'd then go and make it for me. On this day however, as one of the Army's newest officers, when asked if I wanted a brew, with my usual reply of 'yes please', he responded, 'then go and make it yourself, I don't make coffee for officers'.

I have never in my life met someone like Jack. From the moment I saw him at the airport that day, my respect for him has never wavered. I just wish I had a photo of us together. I want him to work within 100%—he would be a brilliant fit. When that day comes, I will finally get that photo.

With Dad having just graduated from the Royal Military College, Duntroon. It was one of the happiest days of my life to that point

*The night of my graduation with two men that hold the highest levels of my respect,
my dad and Terry Connor - one raised me to be a man,
one trained me to be a soldier.*

IT'S NOT A JOB, IT'S AN ADVENTURE

'It's not a job, it's an adventure'
The character Casey Ryback
from the movie *Under Siege*

One thing being in the Army gave me was some amazing opportunities. I travelled the world, I lived in different cultures, and I fired a lot of different weapon systems. I played with a lot of expensive toys, like armoured personnel carriers, tanks, and artillery—to name merely a few.

The training environment at RMC had stolen my confidence, I wasn't the same confident man who'd joined. With the high attrition rate at the college, I'd spent 18 months in training stressed out of my mind. I never relaxed, the place gave me anxiety, it still does. Even 20 years later I feel my body change when I walk through the gate and onto the grounds. When I graduated, joining the Army proper, it made me shine! It gave me back my confidence.

There's a lot to be gained when you find yourself naturally good at something. I was a long way from the best junior officer, but I threw everything I had at my career, education, and training. Confidently discovering I was a lot better than average as a junior officer—I was loving life and in my dream job.

What I learned over the following 10 years however was that the Army demands you believe in it completely. It will offer you so much, but it will demand you give it ten times what it gives you—are you willing to sacrifice your personal relationships and your professional life through less-than-desired postings for the betterment of the Army? Because that's what it's demanding.

I had many thankless days and weeks on end that would give me little to no reward. Opportunities were given to people I believed were less deserving than I was, and I saw people more deserving also missing out— that became my way of holding it together; I always believed that my chance would come. What I learned however was that time, life and opportunities wait for nobody and sometimes these opportunities will come and be gone before you realise what happened.

They say there are two times when the enemy attacks—when you're ready and when you're not, so always be ready, opportunities are the same. Make sure when that opportunity presents itself in the distance that you're prepared to go and get it. If you're lucky enough and it comes to you, take it! I found the people who took opportunities or placed themselves in a position for them to present were far happier in the Army than the ones who did little for themselves. I noticed some people developed a 'victim mentality' becoming scorned and discontent. I always asked, were they willing to give more to get more, or were they just there making up the numbers? It's been said many times to lead, follow or get out of the way, and this was what the Army was to me, a place where your career could thrive or a place where your career would die, a dog-eat-dog environment.

I was in my Engineer basic training in Sydney when those of us posted to the 1st Combat Engineer Regiment in Darwin met with our Commanding Officer. He, by chance, happened to be in Sydney for a series of meetings and came to see us. One of his agenda items was working out which of us would command which Troop (Think Platoon of soldiers) the following year. Three of our group would only have one year as Troop Commanders— they were senior and the remaining three of us would have a second year.

We decided as a group that the ones with only one year should get the Troops likely to deploy to East Timor. Their opportunities to command on operations were fewer than ours.

Now I stand by this decision, but a part of me wishes the Commanding Officer chose who would take which position himself, based on merit. One of the guys, a highly intelligent officer was offered the Troop we all knew would deploy to East Timor, the other two took the Troops they wanted—they made their choices. The three of us who had a second year, we were offered the remainder.

My assigned Troop had some amazing guys, and I learnt an awful lot from them, not only as an officer, but as a man and a leader, I never regretted this decision.

Years later, when it was being decided at a different Army unit who would go to Afghanistan, some of the same people who were a part of this earlier decision were once again in contention for this deployment.

I loved commanding of Armoured Personnel Carriers. It was tough and it was challenging, which is why I loved it so much.

The chosen officer on this occasion was rightly given on merit; he also happened to be the same officer we helped facilitate taking command of the Troop that deployed to East Timor.

We were in the Officers' dining room one day when he started to tell us how amazing he was, that he'd been to East Timor and was now going to Afghanistan—the rest of us had done nothing. I quickly reminded him of the conversation years earlier, when as an act of good faith, myself along with the others had gifted him that opportunity by not competing for it. It made me realise that people will always remember the things you did wrong by them, but they may choose to remember the things you did right by them. I had to check myself and knew, that if I worked hard and an opportunity like this presented again, I'd be ready to attack it; I wasn't playing nice anymore. I wasn't about to walk over people to get it, but I would no longer do what I thought to be better for them and their careers at my own expense. This would prove to be the right attitude. Three months later, that knock at the door came—I was ready!

I deployed to Afghanistan on 03 January 2006. It was the day after the Cronulla riots, and it was 43 degrees. I departed Sydney International Airport headed to Afghanistan, first stop, Perth; from Perth we stopped to refuel at Diego Garcia, a tiny Island in the Indian Ocean that is a part of the United Kingdom. Next stop, Kuwait.

We arrived in Kuwait mid-morning and after some initial briefs made the short journey by bus to the local holding base. It was like you would see in a movie, with American vehicles and armed personnel 'hut-hut-hutting' and running all about the place—it was really like a beehive of activity. We were taken to the Australian compound and given a brief on where the places we needed to know were. We were told that the DFAC (Dining Facility) was behind KFC and Pizza Hut and adjacent to the Golden Arches and on the opposite side of the Green Beans coffee shop—surely not, as I turned to see the golden arches—it was next level. Here I was in a holding area, between two separate war zones—namely Iraq and Afghanistan—and I could get a Big Mac!

I spent a few days receiving briefs on what to expect. Some of the necessary briefs we'd received in Australia prior to deploying were by specialists in their field. The two that are at the forefront of my mind are the one on the culture, presented by an Afghani doctor, who now worked in Sydney as a taxi driver. The other on what to expect if captured by our enemy. I recall thinking this would be interesting; as it turns out it was, but not for the reasons I'd first believed.

We knew if captured by our enemy the only information we could offer was our name, rank, date-of-birth, and our Army number. We knew we'd be beaten, and we knew we'd be tortured—we were fine with that. We knew to humanise ourselves as much as we could with our captors, all while remaining within the lines of operational security. If forced to do a video in captivity, we'd previously completed a series of personalised messages we'd say and or actions we'd make to show we were ok. Mine was to talk about Mickey (my dead childhood budgie) or I would tell Kate, (my late grandmother) that I loved her. I would also rub my eyebrow with a thumb or scratch the side of my chin with four fingers as a physical sign. I would not however rub my nose with a thumb and index finger—I do this naturally. The other actions were less natural for me, and I would have to think to do these. I didn't want to be accidently rubbing my nose and have people thinking I was fine when really, I was anything but.

What they were to say next for many of us was the shocking part, 'In the event that you are captured, you will be raped. Now men, if two or more of you are captured and they are raping one of you in front of the other, don't be surprised if he gets an erection and or if he ejaculates, this doesn't mean he's liking it, this is physiologically a natural reaction, there is nothing he can do about it, nobody gets excited, or likes being raped'. The silence in the room was deafening. I was thinking, man, that really escalated fast! Some of the boys were talking about keeping a spare bullet for themselves if they were captured so as to not be raped. I was just thinking 'don't get captured'.

Possibly the funniest brief I was to receive was from an Australian soldier in Kuwait. Here I was in a classroom of close to 100 of the hardest men you would ever find in a room. Filled with Special Forces Operators from both the Australian Special Air Service Regiment and the 4th Battalion, The Royal Australian Regiment (Commando), this female Private soldier from the Royal Australian Corps of Transport was briefing us on the safety requirements while travelling in a convoy of buses.

I felt for her, she was tasked with giving this brief by her superiors and told that she wasn't allowed to change it in any way to suit her audience.

She briefed that she was the nominated person who would carry the singular weapon for the convoy, explaining how and when she would implement this weapon system. You could hear the snickers from her audience. She looked up at these hardened men, and the reality of the brief said, 'or one of you can have it and do it, you would probably do a better job anyway'. A reply came from the back of the room 'it won't get to that point', the room filled with laughter—even from her. I saw her later at the dining hall and simply said to her 'tough brief', she replied 'the hardest'.

Afghanistan was some of the best and worst times of my life. I loved almost every minute of it: I was doing what I had been trained to do. If you look throughout most professions, they are trained to do their job, and they do it daily. Think of the police, fire brigade, and ambulance—they're trained and are then on the frontline every day. Here I was six years deep into a career and this was the first time I would do my job for real. This wasn't a training exercise, which we completed a lot of in the Army. This wasn't a course, which we also did many—this was the real deal, and for the next five months I got to do my job—the one I was trained for, day in and day out. I loved it.

I was sent to be the commander of the Explosive Ordnance Disposal team, searching for and doing everything that we could to keep our force element safe from explosives.

Additionally, as I was at the time an Engineering Officer, I was given the responsibility to manage and lead the tradesmen who had been sent to maintain the camp—a carpenter, a plumber, an electrician, a plant operator and a soldier who was the odd jobs man. While I loved them all, there were times, some of them made life as the boss really difficult, fighting me constantly on daily taskings. In my mind they'd forgotten that they were a soldier first, an engineer second and a tradesman third—in some of their minds they were a tradie first and to hell with the rest, that's not why I'm here—I couldn't have disagreed with them more.

On one occasion, all the force element 'fighters' were out of the compound, patrolling, gathering information and looking for bad guys. They were as we would say, 'outside of the wire', or off base. A large group of locals were observed to be massing, not more than five kilometres from the base—we didn't know who they were or what they were doing. The bosses, still 'inside the wire' wanted to know; they were adamant they were going to find out.

Previously we had been notified in an intelligence report that there were up to 5000 men who wanted to attack us, was this them? We didn't know, but noting my team were the next choice to do something about it, I was called to the main office and given ten minutes to be on my way to see who they were and what they were up to.

I called the boys together, and told them who was getting into each of the two cars that we'd been allocated, advising them that I'd give them orders on the move—we didn't have time, we had to get moving. The boys were keen, that is, all bar one, one of the tradies blatantly refused to get into a car, telling me what his job was. I gave him the soldier first mantra and he blatantly refused, saying 'I didn't come here for this', I disagreed, and not having time to argue with him, I got into the car and told him that we'd deal with this when we got back. To me, he had refused to follow a direct order on operations, and therefore he should be sent home, it was black and white in my mind; it was mutiny, which in the early years was punishable by death.

We drove out of the gate and I gave the most important, yet the shortest set of orders I would ever give. I had little information to go off, but here we go, I got on the radio. 'Situation, approximately five hundred people grouping in vicinity of (and gave the location) approximately five kilometres from our location. Their disposition is unknown, their intent is unknown, their actions on are unknown, possible weapon systems are unknown, we are going to check it out. My guidance to you is, if in doubt, shoot it, we will deal with the consequences later, questions?'

There were no questions. We drove in what formation we could with two cars directly towards the group.

As we approached from about two kilometres out, the people seemed to scramble, moving in various directions—they just disappeared, we had no idea where. We set up a tight position and got out to have a look. There were no cave systems that we could see, there were no houses or buildings in the immediate vicinity, they were just gone—it was bizarre. I radioed back with this information and said I felt vulnerable. If they were able to disappear so quickly, they could re-group equally as fast too, we could be severely outnumbered and caught by surprise from several directions.

I positioned the cars in an L shape, so each of the two guns in each car was able to support the other guns and the other car, no matter the possible direction of assault on us. It was at this time that the radio called for me, I was told to search the local area and knock on some doors or do a 'soft knock'; that's one where you are seeking permission to search their premises, not kicking the door in like you would see in the movies, which is a 'hard knock'.

Now here is the issue for these people: we were asking for their permission, and they could have said no, but they knew their saying no would raise a lot of suspicion, suspicion in a place where they really don't want to raise any. So, we drove to the houses that were all spaced at least a kilometre apart, we asked permission, and we searched them. One man was really unhappy about it but allowed us inside his compound, where he had the largest and angriest dog that I had ever seen. It was tied up next to a pile of hay that made no logical sense in where it was placed. Further, he had women in the house, this is where this can be really sensitive. A man is not allowed to look at, let alone search a woman, so we came up with a plan for how we could search his house without having to look at or touch the ladies.

The hay was searched, but to do so we 'asked' (read made), the man hold his dog back. The dog was going insane, the man screamed at us to search the hay pile faster; one of the boys poked at the hay, hoping that what he was poking wouldn't explode. The dog, whose paws were on the man's shoulders and the man's head planted firmly in the dog's chest, with the dog's head about two feet higher than his, it was losing its mind—I made sure that I stayed far enough away that even if released, the dog's tether would stop it from getting to me—I also wasn't content that the tether wouldn't rip out of the wall. I kept my distance. Having satisfied that there was nothing or nobody untoward, that is what we could tell within the limited time we had, we left the house and made our way to the next place, heading back to camp when we were done—we had no answers. We had no idea who they were or what they were intending. The biggest mystery was where the hell did they all disappear to?

When we returned to camp, the tradesman who didn't come with us, apologised and said that it wouldn't happen again; he'd had time to think about it—fortunately for him, his trade was essential, and we didn't have time to send him home and wait for a new person to arrive. The other tradesmen in the team wanted more of this, they were primed and ready to go. The electrician loved it, he was sent on a few American patrols to help them—he really got into it.

A month or so later, I happened to be coming off my shift of being on watch. As I walked backed to my accommodation, I noticed that the lights were on in the medical centre. When this happened, you could be guaranteed of a few things. For one, my night vision goggles needed new batteries and they would have batteries available, plus they would always have a coffee on, and they usually had Tim Tam biscuits. A lot of the time, they were watching the TV show '*Scrubs*'—they loved that show, I guess to them it was light-hearted relief. On this night however, when I walked in, they all looked at me wide eyed and seemed happy to see me. They were waiting for local casualties who were soon to arrive on a helicopter, these people needed to be searched and I was now there to do it for them.

I won't go into too much detail, but there'd been an incident involving two young boys and a landmine. They both arrived with the father of one of them. One had lost a leg and the other had substantial facial and head injuries. This was to be a lesson for me on the value of life.

The surgeon looked at the father and through an interpreter said, 'your son has lost his leg, I am going to try to save his life'. As calm as you like the father nodded and said back through the interpreter, 'thank you'. That was it! He looked genuinely appreciative. To him this was no worse than a sprain. I was fascinated. It made me think of home and taking my then, four-year-old daughter Abbey to the emergency room—she had split her head open at pre-school. On this day, people were running around everywhere, making a fuss, especially Abbey—understandable when you are four years old, and your skull shows through the wound. I will give her some credit, it would have hurt, it would have been a shock: but this was another dimension, a lost leg, and massive facial injuries and not a word, not a scream, not a peep. I've seen and heard a lot worse having to deal with a splinter from my kids.

Afghanistan was an amazing experience and one that will remain with me for life, but it doesn't count as the highlight of my service career, it's not even close; that was a real-time job we escalated for in Australia that didn't even happen.

The thought of protecting my fellow countrymen and women in Australia was a far greater thrill to me. I felt like I was actually contributing to what I had signed up to do, 'protect Australia and its interests'.

TOUGH TIMES NEVER LAST, TOUGH PEOPLE DO

'If you think you're going through hell, keep going!'
Winston Churchill.

I t was during my following posting that I reflected upon my previous work within the special forces' community. I applied to do the Special Air Service selection course and had begun preparing. When I look back now, I know I was under prepared. With a heavy workload at the Australian Defence Force Academy (ADFA), I was doing all the training I could within my available time.

I tried my best to replicate the fatigue I would be under on the course, carrying the loads I would be required to carry. Each week in and around the 14-hour days I was working, I trained. This training included a lot of cardio and strength work, in addition to a lot of walking with a heavy pack. I was building to carrying 40—50kg in my pack for up to six hours at a time. While I was fit and strong, I knew I was still underprepared to successfully complete the rigors of the course.

With six weeks until the commencement of the course, I was at a critical point with my training. It was now vital I did the hard work—time was against me. In an attempt to ramp it up to a higher level, there was a risk that my method of training may fail: was the risk worth the reward? It wouldn't be long before the answer came.

I recall the day well, it was a Saturday night, I was working at home. It was just before midnight when I went to bed, waking at 2am and eating left-over spaghetti. I put my pack on and was out the door well before 3am, 60kg on my back, and carrying my steel bar to replicate a rifle. I chose to increase the time, that day I would do a ten-hour walk.

I walked towards Lake Burley Griffin, passing over the Kings Avenue bridge before walking towards Duntroon. Today I would pass through ADFA and make the steep climb up Mount Ainslie, up and over Mount Majura, prior to walking back over Mount Ainslie then walking towards and over Black Mountain—home to the 'Telstra Tower'. After completing this route, I would walk home for a rest prior to completing a recovery session.

As I reached Duntroon I felt considerable pain in the middle of my left foot. With the sun beginning to rise and the first light of the day coming onto my face, I crossed the road and walked up the slight incline towards the headquarters building, I could make out the Corps badges of the 'Badge Gates'. I started to feel sorry for myself. Was it because of the pain I felt? Was it fatigue? Was it the fact that I knew most of the city was still in bed on a Sunday? Was it all the above? I didn't know.

I touched the badges that meant something to me, namely the Engineer and the Infantry badges and I walked off, willing myself to continue, telling myself that its times like this where you make the most progress—when you're working, and the others aren't. I said to myself 'come on mate, you can do this', this is the discipline required—discipline in this instance being the attributes you display when nobody is watching you.

I really wanted to convince myself, that not only did I want it enough, but was I worthy. I'd seen first-hand the life that I would lead in the special force's community, and I'd seen the absolute dedication and professionalism required to be a member. I knew I had it, but would I be able to give enough of myself to achieve it? I knew I wanted it, but I also knew that wanting it sometimes still isn't enough. I pressed on.

I had travelled no more than a kilometre when I walked through ADFA and past where I'd parked my car earlier that week. The level of discipline it took to walk past it was about as deep as I've ever dug. Again, I pressed on. I walked no more than another kilometre when my foot decided that was as far as I was walking that day.

I was gutted, I felt like I'd failed my own session. If I couldn't complete my own mission, how would I complete other missions given to me? The ones that seem so absurd they make you question your ability; the intent of this morning's session was to replicate this. I dropped my pack and once again felt sorry for myself, sitting on my pack with my hands covering my defeated face.

I took a moment and made the decision—I would return to the car, drive home and go for a light run. I wanted to give myself a victory, albeit a minor one. The pain when I stood up was intolerable, picking up my pack and putting it on my back, even worse. I gritted my teeth and began a slow walk back to the car, watching the tray of my ute drop from the weight as I loaded my pack. I drove to the apartment, changed into running clothes, believing my foot would feel better wearing a cushioned running shoe. I was 100 metres into my run when I was having my second self-discussion that day on want, desire, and physical ability.

I rested it for a week, believing whatever was causing the pain would dissipate. I would do strength and water-based training in the meantime, allowing all time I could spare for it to repair. It didn't. A week more and now only a month from the start of selection, I needed it fixed. The stress of starting the course is bad enough, but already feeling under-prepared, I was nervous. I did what I should have done earlier, I went to the medical centre.

Being a staff member of ADFA, specifically in the position I held, I had a lot to do with the doctors in the medical centre, I knew them quite well. I saw Doctor Mark, he's a great man, he and I got along well. He knew what I was training for but didn't really understand what was required to start the course, let alone complete it—I explained it to him. He sent me for an x-ray and not more than 30 minutes later, my hope of starting the course was over. I had a centimetre long stress fracture that went through the entirety of the bone—I was at risk of breaking it completely. My day was done, the risk of injury against the reward of being ready had been won by injury. On this day more than ever came the lesson of minor progressions in training with long and slow increments. I reflected on the lesson, 'if a short cut was really a short cut, it would be the way'. I had tried to do too much on a short preparation—I failed. I was devastated.

Mum has always said that everything happens for a reason, and that a lot of the time, you may never know what that reason is. I wondered what the reason for this could be.

Having broken my foot, I took the time to rehabilitate and recover, getting back to running and starting pack walks again.

I had over a year to be ready for the next course. Time was now my friend, and my motivation was at an all-time high. To start this campaign I kept my training short and light, I did my best to make it fun. I trained a lot and was getting fitter, the daily push towards my long-term goal was back on track.

Fast forward that year, I was fit, I was healthy, and I'd completed considerable educational and psychological training in addition to the physical—I was ready. The day to fly to Perth for the

Happy and ready! The night before I left for the SAS Selection Course, I was fit, I was mentally prepared, and I was ready. What I didn't know, was what would unfold and how my life would begin to change direction. A life of adventure was on the doorstep.

commencement of the Special Air Service Selection Course was here. This was a big day; I was up early and at the airport with the six or so other locals on the course. We flew through Melbourne on our way to Perth for what would be three weeks of pain, discomfort and a lot of unknowns.

We landed in Perth and by the look of the people laying on the ground against their packs, we were the last to arrive. I recall standing at the baggage claim and as soon as my pack came, I was told to move outside and get onto the waiting busses. I threw my pack under a bus and stepped on, not knowing what the next destination would be—would it be Swanbourne, Lancelin or Bindoon? Time would tell.

With this course, you just didn't know what was going to happen. We drove to the local Air Force Base in Perth to see other busses inside a hangar and told to wait. We waited for close to three hours with no information.

A few things happen to you at this point, having just got off a plane, rushed to a loaded bus, then sitting in a hangar with 50-odd rather large heat-emitting, extremely fit humans with no water—you start to dehydrate! We were told to get into PT clothes and wait. A while later we were rushed to another location and told to form up, we'd warm up for the first of our tests, the fitness test!

I'd done a lot of training to this point, and I can say with certainty that the warm-up was hard. Was it anxiety, nerves, dehydration, stress, or all the above? What I know is I was cooked before the actual test started.

We moved to a start point and told that we'd do a run, a man yelled go and I followed the crowd to an unknown destination. One thing I did know was that I was deep into my 'red zone' and the course was only minutes old. We ran to a turnaround point, a man there watching was giving times—four minutes as I turned. Ok, I said to myself, we're doing a 2.4km run. The run back to the start point took a little more out of me than the run there, but I was in the front third of the pack, crossing the line and being given a time of 8:15. My pass mark for this run in the 'regular Army' was just over 11 minutes.

We were told to form up again, this time for a chin up test (heaves as they are called in the Army, always with your palms facing away from you). The pass mark for this test was ten. I found myself in the last rank, I knew I was ready, I'd been doing 'reps' of 25 in training. Rank after rank went through with soldiers from the regiment (called DS for Directing Staff) counting, they seemed to be harsh in their counting, but I expected this, it's all a part of the 'game'.

My turn—nervous, confident and with sweaty palms I held onto the bar, which I was able to hold by standing, the smaller candidates having to jump. 'Begin' is called and I start to pull my body or 'heave' it to the bar, chin over the bar, to hear my counter say, 'don't count that one'. I'm thinking 'it's all a part of the game, just keep going, you have enough interest to get way past ten'. I complete another to hear again, 'don't count that one, your feet touched the ground' then, 'don't count that one, chin too low'. I know I'm pulling myself high enough, my chest was touching the bar, but still, it's the 'game'. I pressed on.

A lot of people struggle to do one military style chin up, and here I have to do ten to pass. I am now at a legitimate 14 completed repetitions, and in the eyes of the DS, I am still on zero. This means that I now have to complete 24 just to pass. I hear him start to count, one, two, three, four, five—I gritted my teeth and pressed on. I don't recall hearing anymore, but I remember heaving my now ridiculously heavy body up one more time to hear the magic word, ten. One more time, eleven and I drop off the bar. My arms, chest and back were on fire.

We turned around to face our counter to watch them call out what the candidate who stood in front of them achieved. There were a lot of high numbers like 17, 22, etcetera, when my DS yelled '11', people were looking at me. Having called out my score, he looked me dead in the eye like a laser and said, 'is that right candidate?' It's a test I tell myself. 'Yes sir' my reply. I'm not about to lose my cool; I passed, who cares the number. I got a P, and P is a Pass. We moved on.

Next was push ups. In the regular army 40 push ups is a pass; here it will be 60. I have been doing sets of 100 in training—I'm confident. Being in the last rank, I believed I had plenty of time to recover, so far so good I was thinking, just pass each test.

With my body still flush with lactate from the heaves, I hear the words, 'back rank, turn around, push up position, ready' WHAT?! They're now going in reverse order, and we got the least amount of rest? No way! Ok— this is going to hurt. Just bang out 60 quick push ups before the fatigue that I am feeling realises what's happened. Then it happens, 'listen to the tape, follow the cadence and don't get in front of it.' NO EFFING WAY! They're doing it to a cadence, I now have to follow the push up, lower, raise, pause for the beep, lower, raise, pause for the beep cadence, not do 60 as fast as I can which was my plan, this one is going to hurt a lot, I was in a lot of trouble. The test began, I lowered my aching body to the ground to make sure that my upper arms were parallel with the ground, I raised until my elbows were locked, every push up was being closely monitored for completion to their satisfaction.

The next few minutes were a messy blur, a blur that I still would rather not think about because I hate failing, even if it's in my own mind. I got to 59 and fought through to 60. Push up number 61 was a mess, at number 62 I was told to stop. There were not many still going in my rank at that point, we would have to wait and see what the others in the following ranks would produce. Apparently, a lot more than we did—the additional rest time had served them well.

We did the sit up test, we all got to 100, moving to a swimming pool for the special forces swim test. I knew this would bring me to the front of the pack, as I swim reasonably well. When I got to the pool, a mate whom I had trained with at Duntroon was there. It had been months since we'd seen one another and this was the first chance we'd had to talk, albeit secretly—there was to be no talking. He would be my lap counter. We started in the pool— just before I dived in, he mouthed the words 'it's cold'.

As I dived in and the water hit my body, I felt my glands move as a team of one towards the collection point in my throat. Holy crap, this isn't cold, this is a word other than that; cold would think that this was cold. Only one way to warm up, start swimming. We did two minutes of treading water to start the test, then swam 400m in 11 minutes to pass, fully clothed in our Army uniforms, including boots.

I turned my pockets out as I treaded water, I didn't want water collection points in my clothing making it harder to swim. We began swimming. I put my head down and started to freestyle, everyone else in the pool besides one other candidate was breast stroking. I swam on. I had my plan—one lap freestyle, one lap breaststroke, which I did, that's until I saw the only other guy that was doing freestyle, tumble turn, kick off the wall and swim back in the opposite direction. OK, freestyle without the impressive turns it was for me then.

Lap after lap I felt strong, while I fatigued a little it wasn't too bad, I got to the wall once again, my mate yelled the lap number to me—I had two laps to go. I see the freak swimmer coming into finish, I finished about a minute or so later. I don't recall the time, but I know we beat the time and the others by a lot. He and I were allowed to get out of the pool but were instructed to wait for the others to finish before we were allowed to change out of our cold and wet clothes—for now, we stood there cuddling to stay warm, waiting for the next people to get out and join the growing group hug.

Back onto the bus and given paper to write an essay on why we wanted to be in the SAS—this was completed while we were driven to another destination. While sleepy and in a hot bus, we were instructed to stay awake, which we did. We arrived at another location; at the time I had no idea where we were. People were looking for their packs and duffel bags which were thrown into a pile, when suddenly, the group took off, following one of the DS.

We walked at a ridiculous pace for what seemed like an hour, still with no water in our water bottles. We arrived at a massive shed that had a bright light beaming out of it. As our watches were taken off us earlier, I had no idea of the time, but I would have guessed it to be close to 10pm. I was one of the last to find my pack, so I was one of the last to arrive to the shed, and therefore I was one of the last to be processed into the building. Prior to being allowed in, we were marked off a sheet, assigned a number—I was given number 12—a photo taken of me holding this number, and led into the building. As candidate number 12, I took my place between guys with the surnames Harvey and Keam. They were candidates 11 and 13.

We were instructed to undress, completely naked. We would all dress piece by piece in the manner they wanted us to. The room was filled with people walking around looking us up and down. Some were men, some men with attack dogs that seemed to stop right next to your privates—there were a lot of women too, some of whom were looking at you and snickering prior to walking off.

Piece by piece we dressed, one sock, then another, then an undershirt, then your camouflage shirt, then the most important piece of equipment you need, I was thinking jocks, but apparently it was my 'I want to quit form'. This was to be placed in your left breast pocket and was to be always on you. In your right pocket was a compass and you were to always have a pen and a notebook on you. Then came jocks, trousers, and shoes.

Dressed it was time to pack our packs, that is how they wanted them packed. We'd been given a list of items to bring, these now lay on the ground in front of us. Harvey didn't bring an item, it's what we call a 'cups canteen' (a steel cup), we'd been instructed to bring two. When questioned to why he hadn't brought them, he stated, 'I don't use them sir'. Now here I am thinking a few things, for one, you want to be one of these guys, they have given you a list of equipment to bring, play the game. As the DS en-masse began yelling at him and making notes in their notebooks. I was thinking 'oh man, you're standing too close to me, I'm feeling the heat on me that you're bringing to yourself', you're too close, I don't need them angry at you, then looking next door to me. Fortunately, they didn't.

The next few days were a bit of a blur, they seemed to all blend into one another, but one thing I knew was that my body was working overtime and that I really saw the best and worst in people. You're told at the outset that you're not competing against anyone else; you're all being assessed, reviewed, critiqued or whatever word you want to use, against yourself. There are no 'quotas', no specific number of places to be filled; you are either deemed suitable for further training, or you're not—pretty simple.

The thing is, when you get a few hundred of the hardest alpha males in the same place at the same time, all with the same goal, you quickly see who gets it and who doesn't. We were each placed into sections of about ten men. My section had me as the only officer. How did I know they were soldiers? Your candidate number was the give-away. The officers were all low numbers and the guys in my section were all numbered into the hundreds.

It was interesting to see how little they wanted to help. We did a navigation exercise, and the candidate doing the navigating had to carry

I'd been training for this moment my entire life. I was on the course that would set up the remainder of my life, just not in the way I planned.

a radio (think backpack size). I watched the other candidates stare at this guy struggling to get it on his back. I walked over and helped him and told the others who were closer they should have helped; they just saw everyone as their competition—they weren't helping anybody. The problem was, by not helping and not having a 'team' mentality, they were defeating themselves. A team mentality with a mission focus is what the regiment desires above all else.

On the third night when we were walking through the bush, I was at the back of the line. My 'team' didn't pass back messages to say there were low or spiky branches: rather they would walk past, hold a spiky branch at full tension and let it swing back into your face. I personally would have held it for everyone to walk through or passed a message back to the next guy. These men were what we would call in the Army as 'Jack' (not doing the right thing by you). This happened at least half a dozen times, and I was over them—I was just so frustrated with them, I hated them.

Add to this, it had been raining since we arrived, the hardest rain you have ever seen. It was so bad that our camp had literally washed away. My stretcher was a long way away from where I'd left it. A decision was made to move the course inside. This had never happened before in the history of the course.

My team were so bad that they refused to talk to one another and wouldn't help at all. The following night, it was dark, and we were moving fast. You didn't have time to look out for yourself, so you relied on the person in front of you to guide the way. The guy in front of me didn't communicate with me, this led me to tripping and falling off a ledge about the height of the roof of a house. I landed between my head and my shoulder, my feet in the air, carrying my pack and equipment. I hit the ground so hard that it took the wind out of me, my shoulder was out, my thumb from the force of my rifle driving into the ground was sideways and my back felt strange. I rolled to take my pack off and get up in one motion, my shoulder clicking back into place. The relief in pain to my shoulder was instantaneous.

I looked at my disfigured hand, clenched my teeth, taking my sideways thumb and pulling it forwards, feeling for the joint and the socket to align, and letting it drop back into place. My back was done, something bad was wrong with it.

I walked back to the building where we were now staying. My DS asked where I had been; I said that I'd fallen over and had to catch up. He mumbled something and walked away. I went inside, my back was in considerable pain.

Now I don't know if you have ever had back pain, but it wrecks your day. Smiling seems to hurt. Every time you move, it hurts—you can't sleep, you can't sneeze, you can't do anything. When you have a broken arm, people can see the cast and know you have a broken arm. When you have back pain, people don't sympathise as they can't see the injury.

The following day it was heavy backpacks on. We had a 20 kilometre walk to do in 3 hours and 20 minutes—something I could normally eat up in my sleep. Our packs were to weigh 20kg, our webbing (fighting belt) 8kg and we carried our rifles. This is something that I had done literally hundreds of times in training; you have to walk fast to meet the time. There was a set of scales to weigh your things at camp and a set at the finish of the walk. I weighed my pack, 22 kilograms, I weighed my webbing, 10 kilograms. With equipment having to weight 28 kilograms in total at the finish, this would allow me to drink four litres of water and still be on weight at the finish. Perfect.

We trucked to the start point, my back jarring with every bounce of the dirt road. Commencing with the lowest candidate numbers I was off in the first group, feeling as well as could be expected. I would get no sympathy here today, not that I wanted any. I would have walked for an hour, a third of the way, when suddenly, what felt like lightning went through my body and I couldn't move the way my body should. I was now taking the smallest steps imaginable, that's all my body would allow. For the next 13 kilometres I walked with a third of my leg stride.

This is something I'd never considered until this point. The smaller your step, the more contact your webbing belt from your equipment has with the cheeks of your butt. The longer your step, the more it slides across a wider section of your bum. Add to this, noting it'd rained for four days leading into this, everything I owned and wore was wet. Damp plus friction, equals burn. The longer the walk takes you, the bigger the burn.

While training for the course, I'd used methylated spirits (watered down in a spray bottle) on my feet every day. This hardens your feet and prevents the likelihood of blisters. Your feet are your life on this course, it's best you prepare them, nobody wants to succumb to the 'I want to quit form' for blisters. Not in one million years would I have thought that I should have toughened my tushy.

I finished the walk, my body and my back now screaming at me due to the inability to walk properly. It took me an additional 30 minutes to finish beyond the time I wanted worst case! I was asked why it had taken so long and informed that I had to re-do and pass that entire walk at a later stage, just to stay on the course. Seemed right to me. I just hoped my back had improved by then. Deep down I knew I was done, but still I asked to see the doctor. The doctor came, asking the standard questions and asked me to touch my toes. I couldn't bend at all; I couldn't touch my knees. I tried again, and again in vain—nothing. I was told that I was ok and that I would be able to continue, with no offer of pain relief. I changed and went to the next task.

I walked outside to join the teams preparing for PT, this would test my back—truck tyre flipping. I was about twenty seconds into this session when I was being yelled at for not being able to do it—remember, you can't see back pain. I walked off to the side, followed by a DS who yelled at me. I told him that my back was no good, and I needed a minute to come to terms with something. He looked at me oddly as I turned and walked away from him. He followed me and I repeated, I need a minute to come to terms with something; this time he watched and waited.

It was in this minute I thought of all the work, time and sacrifice I had put into this venture. I had given so much of myself, I had trained so hard. I had forgone time with my kids and was willing to forgo even more for this life. I had studied, I had learnt palindromes and anagrams. I had refined knots, lashings, tactics and for what, a simple fall. I considered seeing if I could get back into it, recollecting on that day with my foot just over a year earlier. I would try to touch my toes again. This time having cooled down a little, I was even stiffer. I pondered with free medical how much was I willing to hurt myself, so my ego wasn't bruised with a self-withdrawal, the ridicule from others—others who had not had the courage to attempt the course. I thought to myself, 'The lion cares not for the opinion of the sheep'. I walked over to the DS and said, 'I'm too broken, I can't do what I need to do right now, so I will walk away and come back and fight another day'. Without a word, he handed me an 'I want to quit form'. I signed it and was told to collect my things; I would be met by a car to take me to the hangar.

I arrived at the hangar and was told to place my stretcher next to the last one in the line; there would have been at least 20 to 30 there already. I was shown the showers, I grabbed my towel and some clothes and walked to get clean. It was in this shower that the reality of the burn to my bum was to become a little clearer to me. There were no mirrors in this facility, so I would have to be content for now just knowing that it was sore, the soap let me know too. Having had something to eat, I laid on my stretcher and fell asleep, waking at around 10pm. I opened my eyes, I looked, and my stretcher was nowhere near the end of the line as it was when I fell asleep—I was in the middle. What the hell had happened when I was asleep for there to be so many people withdraw? I guess that session I pulled out of was a good one.

I was moved to a house called 'camp happy' near where the training was occurring; this was torture—I could see the course, I could hear the course and I was watching it happening in front of me. It was horrific watching your dream happen in front of you. I was taken back to see the medical staff, it felt like my bum cheeks were leaking through my bike shorts and my trousers. I stated the problem and was asked to remove my pants. The medical orderly was oblique to me when I took my pants off, the look on his face said a million words.

It's never a good sign when the medic asks you lie on the table and says he'll be back; he wanted to get a doctor. It's a worse sign when the doctor walks into the room and says 'Oh wow! Wait right there—I am going to get my colleagues'. Arriving moments later with a team of people, asking me what had caused this with the tasks we'd been completing. I explained the fall, the back issue, the lightning feeling that shortened my gait and how I was guessing that I now had some sort of blister as a result. His reply was to his colleagues, 'this is what it looks like when people fall off a motorcycle in boardshorts, this is a good third-degree friction burn'. Ok! So that explains a lot. They dressed it and with my newly bandaged derrière. I departed back to 'camp happy' with the other removed candidates.

About an hour later I was told to pack my things, transport had arrived to take me to the airport, I was heading home. Five days after I departed Canberra filled with hopes, dreams, and aspirations it was all over. I packed up, was given my phone and my watch, and directed to a car that would take me to Perth airport. Next stop, the QANTAS club to commiserate.

It's funny when you come off this course; a lot of people have seen your dedication. The people that you love and work with know how much you want it, they can tell. As hard as it is for you to see them, I learned that it's hard for them to see you too. They farewell you and wish you well, not expecting to see you for weeks, and if you're successful, it can be months before you're allowed to go home to pack and move to Perth. But seven days after leaving, I was back at work. Of course, people want to know what happened to you, what made it easier was one of the guys I worked and trained with had dislocated his shoulder the same day that I was injured, he returned to work the same day as me. The fact that two of us went back to work on the same day made it somewhat easier.

Most of my colleagues were sad to see me back, but then there was one guy who seemed somewhat happy; he said, 'I knew you'd fail'. My reply shut him down pretty fast, 'I was candidate number 12, what were you? Oh, that's right, you weren't there, so shut up, you don't know what you're talking about. I'll let the people with the courage to attempt the course judge me, not a fat prick like you'. Of course, there is no response to this, and had he have tried I would have given him some more home truths. I literally had no respect for him—his comment merely one reason why.

The hardest one was a lady who'd been my boss for a short period the year prior. To her, I would have been one of the harder people she commanded. I was from the fighting corps' in the Army, and she was a meteorologist in the Navy—you can't get more removed than this.

I liked her, she didn't try to over command me, she came to understand that I did my job without a need of supervision, and anything she required of me was done on time and on target; she just gave me the rope and I didn't let her down. I learned quickly that she had my back, and she knew that I had hers too. She earned my trust and more to the point, she earned my respect. I recall when she saw me in the hallway that day, she looked shocked. She said, 'I don't know what to say at a time like this' and stood there in disbelief, with her hands open and in front of her. I grabbed her open hands replied, 'that was perfect'. She gave me a hug and I walked away. To this day that lady has my respect, the other bloke has none.

I went to medical to have them assess my back, it was still horrific—the pain unimaginable. At the doctor's request to describe my pain on a scale of one to ten, with ten being intolerable, I said 75! Looking at a mirror I was twisted, I could see the curve in my spine. I had to use wire coat hangers with the hooks through my trouser belt loops to pull my pants up. I needed help to tie my shoes, I couldn't bend at all.

The scans revealed I had misaligned two facet joints in my spine. If you don't know what they are, they're the spiky bits that come off the back of the vertebrae. They have a joint that aids your movement, when misaligned, I can't begin to describe the pain and discomfort. All I can say is there are a lot of nerves in your back, and many of mine were screaming at me. The recovery process was a long one, and my bum, well it had scarring for many years.

I'd already decided that if I didn't get through selection, I would transfer Corps (Army Trade) to the Infantry. They were more 'my people' and to be honest, the Engineer Corps no longer inspired me; I just was no longer interested in anything they did. The Infantry however, it excited me—to me, this was what being in the Army was all about. I had already liaised with the Infantry Career Advisor; I contacted him and wrote a letter that had been endorsed by my boss. Less than a week later the Career Advisor contacted me and asked me if I would go to the 7th Battalion of the Royal Australian Regiment (7 RAR). They were newly created from the de-linked 5th/7th Battalion, with 5 RAR and 7 RAR now individual units. Being a mechanised unit and me coming from a mechanised background, this was a way that I would be able to find my footing and fast.

He contacted me the following day and suggested that I would have to take a cut in my level of seniority. Being a fourth year Captain, I would have to do a suite of roles in the Infantry as a junior officer to build a profile, this was so I was able to compete with my peer group in future years for higher positions. He suggested that I would lose at least three to four years in seniority.

I laughed, 'is that all?', 'I want to be a fourth year Lieutenant' (which is a five-year loss in seniority). Seeming somewhat surprised at my comment, 'What?!' was the reply followed by an inquisitive 'Why?' 'Easy!' I replied, 'If I am a fourth year Lieutenant, I'm able to be a Platoon Commander again, which will tick this box in my new Corps. It will give me a year to make mistakes, and it will allow me to build an even stronger profile. This is not a short-term move'. Confused at my wishes, he told me he'd get back to me, my desire and willingness to do more than he'd suggested had changed everything in his mind; he needed to talk to his boss.

About an hour later the phone rang, it was the Career Advisor again. He said that they had assessed my profile in greater detail and the fact that I was qualified to be a Mechanised Infantry Company Commander, I had been a Troop Commander within Special Operations Command and had deployed to Afghanistan in this role, not only would I not be a Lieutenant, but I would also remain a Captain with no loss of seniority at all. Damn it! It was worth a shot. So, two days after the official paperwork was signed, the Engineer Corps agreed to lose me, the Infantry Corps agreed to take me and I was the day after that, a member of the Royal Australian Regiment. I would however finish my year working at the Defence Academy. My ducks were once again back in a row.

Career wise for me, I was with my peer group. The best performers from my Duntroon class were filling the same appointments in other units around the country as me.

With the daily average temperature in the low fifties, I was taken into the desert, given a compass bearing to follow and a distance to run.

THE DESERT IS YOUR FRIEND

'A rose in the desert can only survive on its strength, not its beauty'
Matshona Dhilwayo

Posted to the 7th Battalion I was once again in an operational unit; I was back to being in the job I craved. I was happy, content and sent on an international course that showed me there was more to the world than the life I was currently living. That said, it wasn't until some reflection much later, that I saw what was so clearly in front of my face.

My first job each morning was to check my emails. I needed to see if there was anything that required immediate action before I could go and train. I had an email that detailed that I, along with another guy from work, had been selected to attend a desert warfare course in Pakistan. 'A what! And where?' This was my initial reaction. I had no idea that someone had nominated me for this course, being made aware of a course nomination is usual practice.

As I investigated a little more, I found out this wasn't a joke, rather, I would in a matter of weeks be sent to Pakistan to live in a village called Chorr (amusingly in the local language, Urdu, this means 'the end of the world'). I would learn to live and fight in the desert. The Australian and Pakistani Governments had agreed to conduct training courses together. You can assess why.

To be ready to go on time, we had a lot of work to do. Firstly, we needed visas to get into the country, with the applications sent to the Pakistani High Commission in Canberra. Now this is where it starts to get weird. The most senior defence member in Pakistan wanted us to fly and meet him in Islamabad before the course started. We would then have to travel to Hyderabad, at the other end of the country. So, with our travel planned for us, we'd fly to Dubai, transfer to Islamabad, fly back out of Pakistan to Dubai, to then fly back to Hyderabad in Pakistan. I too was confused.

When our passports arrived back with our visas, they were permitting only one entry into Pakistan. So, we returned our passports to the High Commission along with a covering letter, seeking to have visas that enabled us to enter the country twice.

When the passports returned to us a matter of days prior to our departure, rather than place a new visa in the passport, the Pakistani High Commission used 'white out' on the original visa and wrote in pen '2' where previously there had been a typed number '1' next to the words 'permitted entries into Pakistan'. There were a lot of concerns, but it had come from the High Commission, so I trusted that I could rely upon being stopped at customs, them contacting the Pakistani High Commission in Canberra and then someone saying 'oh yeah! Those blokes, its ok'. That's what I had in my head anyway.

The day came for us to depart, and we travelled to Dubai with no issues, well not for me anyway. My travel buddies TV didn't work in Business Class, so he was offered a seat in Economy with a functioning TV, that or a bottle of wine as an apology to stay in Business Class—he took the wine.

We had to overnight in Dubai, a hotel had been booked for us. We cleared customs with a little bit of fast talking. While we had accommodation, we weren't really meant to be there, but seeing it was for only one night, customs weren't too concerned.

We went to baggage, where we waited, and waited. We bought a coffee, and waited, and waited some more, when I said, 'bugger it!' and headed to baggage services, where we waited some more again.

We would have been there an hour, looking at a lot of confused people when one of them came back to let us know that our bags had not stopped in Dubai, they hadn't even gone straight through to Islamabad—they were en-route to Hyderabad! That's where we'd be in a week.

With this, we left the airport and made our way to the hotel. I was happy enough, my day pack at least contained a spare shirt, socks, a pair of jocks and a toothbrush with paste.

Driving through Dubai is amazing, I loved it. I swore I'd go back one day, which I am yet to, but I have a lot of exploring to do there.

Arriving at the hotel, we decided to shower, and I would change clothes. We'd then head to the local shopping centre to buy more clothes to get us through the week. We hailed a taxi at the front of the hotel, headed for the local shopping centre—the Dubai Mall.

If you've never heard of the Dubai Mall, it's worth a Google. We walked in open mouthed! There was an Ice-Skating Rink in the middle, massive water features, the largest shops I had ever seen and just so many things to look at. We wandered for what felt like hours, passing through the 'Gold Souk' which is pretty much lines of the biggest jewellery shops in the world, each filled with the biggest gold and diamond products you will ever see. We wandered in and out of every shop in the Gold Souk, believing it all to be reasonably priced from what we could tell from our currency converter. What we didn't know at the time, is that it's illegal for a jewel trader to rip you off—had we have known that I would have been buying a few things!

Leaving the Gold Souk, we saw people walking into the ice rink to skate, yep, we're on! We were straight into the ice rink, skates on and ripping around small Arab kids, having the time of our lives, until we remembered, we hadn't bought any clothes yet! The reason we came here in the first place.

It was skates off and straight to the Billabong outlet where I bought enough things to get me through the week.

The following morning after a lack of sleep thanks to a local Irish Bar, we made our way back to the Dubai International Airport, bound for Islamabad. If I thought getting into Dubai was rough, it was about to get a whole lot worse.

As we flew into Pakistan, what I knew was that we were landing in Rwalpindi, which is a city that bounds Islamabad. Rwalpindi was formerly the Capital, and it was also the place where a former Prime Minister, Benazir Bhutto was assassinated. I was literally about to land at the Benazir Bhutto International Airport.

As we landed, we looked at a scene that resembled the movie '*Slum Dog Millionaire*'. There were armed guards everywhere. We passed through the first check point, where our passports were checked. A smile appeared on the guard's face as he looked at the visa, yet he waved us through.

There's a good point to note at this time. Myself and my travel buddy were a good foot taller than everyone else on the plane. We're white, we're in polo shirts—mine happened to be red. To say that we stood out is an understatement.

We reached the next check point—same thing, but a bigger smile on the guard. Next was immigration; this guy was almost laughing as he waved us through, saying something on his radio as we passed him. We headed towards customs, remembering, we didn't have luggage, just day packs, now bursting with the additional clothes we'd purchased in Dubai.

As we reach customs, the two officers are in the highest of spirits, greeting us into their stall, 'hello gentleman, where have we come from today? The US?' 'No', I reply, 'we're Australian, we transferred through Dubai'. Their smiles seemed to disappear a little and their cocky nature vanished. 'Oh, what is your business here in Pakistan?' 'Where here on the request of the Chief of Army, General Kayani to complete the Army Desert Warfare Course in Chorr'. The mood shifted to almost one of a desire to assist. Our passports were returned, 'have a good day sir, enjoy your stay in Pakistan', we walked off.

Now at this point while I had just seen the power of the Chief of Army in Pakistan, I was also a little concerned. I was yet to see the Australian point-of-contact we'd been assured would be inside of the airport to meet and help us through these predicaments. We walked through more check points now with relevant ease. As we got closer to the outside of the building, the crowds got bigger and louder.

Exiting the airport, there was a mass of people, the kind you would expect for this part of the world—it was chaos!

As we walked out it seemed to go deathly quiet, all faces turning to look at two white guys who stood a lot taller than most. As the crowd went back to its normal state, we stood against a wall, backpacks in hand waiting for someone, something to seem normal and that we were meant to be there.

I decided to go for a walk to see if I could find our contact; my mate stayed in the same place, so I knew where to find him. As I walked around, some people said hello to me, others grunted, and a few started to push me about; I pushed past them. A lot of people offered to drive me where I needed to go—tempted for a millisecond, it just didn't seem safe, I refused.

I made my way back to my travel buddy, and the crowd seemed to almost turn towards us, and on us. They came closer and closer to us and seemed somewhat agitated, almost to the point of violence. I remember thinking there was a good chance I would be murdered on my son's birthday; it wasn't the most pleasurable thought. At least he would remember the day I died.

I turned to my mate, our backs literally against a wall, we were looking at the road with a car park on the other side. At the back of the carpark was a massive billboard, with a Pepsi logo. I said to my mate, 'when I say go, you go left, I'll go right, run like an Olympian, I will meet you at that Pepsi sign on the other side of the car park—we'll sort it out from there'. He agreed.

It was at this point when one of the people said 'we hate American's, were going to cut your head off' I was about to yell go! Then my mate said in a calm and almost concerned manner, 'we're not American, we're Australian'. The reply was something that you would never pick, 'Australian like Ricky Ponting?' 'Yes mate, like Ricky Ponting, Michael Slater, Adam Gilchrist, Matthew Hayden and Brett Lee'. His joy! Our would-be attacker proclaimed to the angry crowd, 'It's OK! They're Australian like Ricky Ponting!' Thank God for Ricky Ponting!

As the crowd dispersed, a black up-armoured BMW pulled up ten metres to our front. It was the Australian contact, who jumped out, said 'you're early, get in' and with that we speed away through the streets of Rwalpindi in an armoured vehicle using infra-red over driving lights.

On arrival at the Australian High Commission, it was made apparent why we'd been requested to arrive here for briefs before heading to Hyderabad. This was the first time this course had been run with international student participation; we were with the first to be invited. There was an emphasis on Australia having more people in and around Pakistan, that is, it borders Afghanistan. Our conduct on the course was to be professional, friendly, and willing to help. The Pakistani Chief of Army pretty much runs the country, he had personally called the Commandant of the Army Desert Warfare School and briefed him to keep us safe.

This all seemed pretty straight forward to me—be a good guy, try hard, and don't compromise safety. Easy!

It was while we were here that one of the funniest moments of my life happened. Our host's wife asked us if we wanted a cup of coffee and how we had it. When we said, 'white and one sugar please', she looked somewhat alarmed, then proclaimed, 'I will get Hassan the house boy, to go and get us some milk'. 'Hassan, can you go and get some fresh milk please?' Now a look of confusion came across Hassan's face, but he replied, 'yesss ma'am' in a long-drawn-out tone as he walked out of the house. She said, 'I really don't know why he seemed so concerned; I mean, there was a shooting at the front of the house a few nights ago, but it's been safe ever since—the shops are close by'.

Hours go by and no Hassan, the mood in the house starts to shift that maybe Hassan's concerns were somewhat justified. It got to the point that our host's wife was about to call our host—he was at work, when Hassan walked through the gate, torn shirt, that was covered in both dirt and blood. He was carrying a plastic bag with milk in it, not in a container in a bag- the bag was the container.

Standing in the Pakistani Desert ready to become the first person in the history of the course to hit all checkpoints, a goal that would change with a checked ego for the betterment of someone else.

It seems the Pakistanis are quite literal, and the use of the term 'fresh milk' had Hassan believe it was to be 'fresh from the cow', not fresh from the shop. Poor bugger, he looked defeated. I can only imagine the trouble he went to, just to find a cow in the city, let alone trying to milk it.

Leaving Islamabad, we transferred back through Dubai and into Hyderabad. Upon our arrival we were faced with a similar situation as when we landed in Rwalpindi, but with a lot more smiling at us this time, that is until we reached customs who wanted to know why the number '2' was in whiteout on our visas. I explained the situation to him, but he wasn't buying it. He passed it up the chain. I am guessing someone ended up calling the Pakistani High Commission in Australia and much like I predicted, someone sitting in Canberra was like 'oh yeah, those guys, they're ok', and we were let in. The reason I hold this belief is that it took about two hours to clear customs.

A day later and we were off to Chorr. It would be a two-day drive through the cities and the country in the back seat of a Toyota Hilux ute, a .50 Calibre machine gun mounted on the roof. A soldier stood in the tray of the ute manning the gun—anytime someone came too close to the car, they had a machine gun pointed at them.

Two days of gridlocked roads filled with cars, donkey carts and fuel trucks with a warning to let everyone know that their load needed to be treated with caution, as it was 'highly inflammable'!

We arrived at the containment where the course would take place. It was situated 30 kilometres from the Indian border, right in the middle of the Thar Desert. Like the name suggested, it did feel like the end of the world.

The course was fine, but it was pretty basic for our rank and experience. Lessons were at a very introductory level. We quickly discovered through observation that the course was a big deal to the Pakistani students, they'd all been selected to represent their parent units.

Each day we had a series of lessons in the morning, with time to study in the afternoon. The navigation was much like our basic training at Duntroon. The only issue I had was with the compasses, they were all old and inaccurate—they were never consistent. I emailed a mate in Australia and asked him to send me a northern hemisphere compass and a camelback water bladder to wear on my back. With the practical navigation to come, I wanted something better than what I had.

No word of a lie, four days later a parcel arrived containing the compass and a camelback. It takes longer to send my kids a card in Queensland, but this thing made it from Perth to the India/ Pakistan border in four days!

My new compasses perfectly timed arrival had me set to commence the assessed practical navigation exercises. With the daily average temperature now in the low fifties Celsius, we were taken into the desert, given a bearing to follow and a distance to travel. When we arrived at this destination, we would be given the next destination to find. We had four hours to complete four legs, briefed that no student in the history of the course had ever completed every leg of every navigational exercise—there would be no fewer than 20 of these exercises on this course.

In pairs we set off! I was with my Australian buddy, and we took off at speed. We knew in the desert, unlike in the bush, we were able to see for miles and miles. This would mean judging the distance would be less important, as we'd be able to see the target in the openness of the desert, something the bush doesn't allow; where if you fail to judge the distance, you may miss a target hidden by foliage.

As we made our way to the first checkpoint, we noticed a soldier armed with a rifle following us. He did his best to maintain pace but fell further and further behind. We believed he was just heading to the same checkpoint as us, but for some reason, as we departed the first checkpoint for the second, with no time to stop and rest, he kept following—he looked hot and flustered.

As we departed the second checkpoint for the third, we realised that the checkpoints were in a box shape. This was further highlighted by the fact that our armed follower didn't go through the second checkpoint—he changed direction and started to run the diagonal within the box from check point two directly to checkpoint four, wanting to arrive with us at the finish of our fourth and final leg, which he timed perfectly—albeit arriving from a different direction. It was obvious to everyone watching that the soldier couldn't maintain our speed—he was therefore no security at all, the very reason we later discovered why he was following us.

As we arrived back at the start point, we noticed that we were close to being the last to arrive. We were confused—nobody was faster than we were, they all seemed to be going in either the same or opposite direction and there was an hour until the cut off time. I had no idea how they'd beaten us.

We were handed a drink and offered some shade to sit, the other students started talking, asking us how many check points we managed to get to, 'four?' My curious reply. There was some commotion within the group and discussions changed from English to Urdu. Interested I asked one of the others how many checkpoints they'd achieved, the main consensus of the group was two, for some it was only one.

I was so confused; I couldn't work out why they failed in checkpoints and not failed in time. Why would they choose to fail and not be out there until the last moment in time, trying to find more? I was at a loss.

I found many of the Pakistani staff and trainees overconfident (read arrogant). They lacked humility and were not a pinch as competent as they believed—their failures highlighting this. The longer the course went on, the more they chose to fail and the more they resented us for getting 100% every time we were given one of these activities. Interestingly, the Pakistani soldiers, not the officers on our course, loved us! They thought we were personable, we spoke to them as equals and they could see that we weren't just talk, we could back it up.

Of interest, after this first navigation exercise, they no longer had a soldier with a rifle follow us for the entire exercise—they had a different

Try explaining to a Bedouin in the middle of the Thar Desert on the Pakistan/
India border what an Australian is. My Mate and me on the Pakistan Army Desert
Warfare Course.

soldier follow us for each leg; they couldn't keep up, that's until they decided to stop having them follow us at all—they weren't recovering in time for the next exercise. I'm not trying to be cocky or arrogant by saying this either, they were just trained differently to us. Our training has a larger emphasis on cardiovascular fitness than theirs. They just didn't run unless they had to, whereas in our Army, people run every day for fun and fitness.

Now with no armed escorts and no longer working in pairs, I loved the individual process. Once again it brought me back to my childhood and my time at Duntroon doing similar activities. I was alone in the wilderness, and I was doing something I loved—this time however, I was exploring in a foreign country. It's on these moments that I now reflect in my current role, with my passion for being in foreign places and being so remote, but here I was, and I was loving it—and still hitting every checkpoint, much to the disgust of the other trainees.

From time to time, I would come across Bedouin villages. The people would look confused at a random white man running through their desert. I would smile and wave and stay on my course; they would just give me strange looks and a random wave back.

On the first solo night navigational exercise, we were driven in trucks for what seemed like an hour. We weren't allowed to know where we were going, nor that it mattered to my mate and I—we had no idea anyway. We were unloaded from the back of the truck and told to hand in our compasses, tonight we'd only be using the stars.

We were all assigned one of four routes, titled A through D. I was given route A and informed that I had to travel 3 kilometres and given a bearing, which was due north. With the moon yet to rise, there was little to no ambient light.

I'd travelled about one and a half kilometres; I could hear nothing, and I could see nothing on the ground, but with no light pollution, the stars filled the sky. I stopped to re-check my direction, which you have to do every 15 minutes when you use the stars. I heard a noise that made no sense—it was like a grunting noise. Then I heard almost a growl, I verbalised 'what the hell' when I heard things far worse than this. A camel charged me! It was tethered but ran straight at me—I dived out of the way and yelled at it, people started yelling and screaming, lights came on in tents and makeshift dwellings all around me—somehow, I had made my way into the centre of their village. I could hear weapons being cocked. I wasn't waiting another second; I got out of there.

As I crested a hill about 500 metres to the north, I could see what looked like a siren light in the distance. It was absolutely in the direction I needed to go to; surely not, surely this wasn't the checkpoint. In Australia there's a 'dog-tag' attached to a pole with no light, this was extremely easy!

The soldier manning the checkpoint was grinning almost hysterically and asked me if I found the village. He said he'd driven around it and realised it was directly on the bearing we'd be taking. He was waiting expectantly, hoping one of the Pakistani students came through first, but found it even funnier that it was me. Honestly, by this stage I did too. I even waited to see who came in after me to see their reaction before I left for my next checkpoint.

Fortunately, it was one of the Pakistanis and not one of the other foreign students invited to attend the course—he said he explained to them who he was and what he was doing, they all calmed down. He mentioned that the hardest thing to explain to them was what an Australian was, having to draw the world on the ground and explaining I was from another country. They seemed quite excited by this—from what I recall, they seemed anything but excited.

The final night exercise came, and we were back to working in pairs. I was back with my Australian mate, and we had five checkpoints to go to be the first to get every checkpoint on the course. He too was yet to miss a checkpoint. While we were excited at the thought, the Pakistani students were filthy about it. We'd made good friends with a British guy who had a Pakistani heritage—he'd joined their Army. He mentioned there had been a meeting between the staff and Pakistani students where the message was, they'd all been completely outclassed and should feel disgraced—two foreign students would be the first to hit every checkpoint.

As we left for the first checkpoint some of them wanted us to help them—we saw what they were doing, we were having none of it. We made our way to our destination using the stars. As we crested a sand dune, we could see the red light in the distance as per normal, but this time, strangely there were two cars—normally there was only one.

As we ran into the checkpoint, the Regimental Sergeant Major (the senior soldier) of the course was there. He told us we were finished for the night and to get into the car—but we still had four to go. He looked us dead in the eye and said, 'sirs, please get in the car. We cannot tell our Chief of Army that you have completed every checkpoint. In the history of this course, nobody, not even I did that, it would be of great embarrassment to the Commandant and all of us if you are the first'.

Humbled, and taking away our desire to 'be the first' we saw the greater good that would come from us failing that night. He asked us once again to get into the car, we refused. We said we understood, but we would not get into the car, that was being defeated; we would walk back to the start point. With a smile he thanked us, shook our hands, and asked if he could walk back with us, 'we would be honoured'.

As we walked back to the start point, he went onto explain more politics within the course. It became clear that we had outperformed the others across the scope of training. He mentioned how impressed he was with our light-hearted attitude and that we were willing to sit and talk with the soldiers, something he had never seen a Pakistani officer do.

Back at the start point, there was food, tea and cordial waiting for us. We sat with the team and then removed ourselves before the other trainees arrived, sitting against a tree with a bush immediately behind it. The Regimental Sergeant Major advised us against sitting where we chose, cobras like to live in the bushes. We laughed—that was until a mongoose ran straight between us and into the bush. Thrashing was heard as we launched from our seat to the roar of laughter from the onlookers.

While this course had its moments, it taught me there was more to life than soldiering. I loved the adventure, and I loved the exploration, I just didn't see how I would be able to do it for a living. What I knew however was that I needed to add more adventure and exploration to my life, even as a hobby.

With New direction and more time for family, I wanted to show them what I had been doing all those years.
With Drew at an Army open day at Enoggera Barracks in Brisbane, where it started all those years prior.

NEW DIRECTIONS

'I can't change the direction of the wind, but I can adjust my sails to reach my destination'

Jimmy Dean

It was during my time as a Company Commander at the 7th Battalion that my eyes widened a little more on progression within the Army. I came to realise that the dedication and commitment against personal sacrifice was now too great for me to seek a future in the 'profession of arms'.

I was missing a lot of the important events in life. My son had turned eight years old, and I was yet to be at home for one of his birthdays. I missed his birth because of the Army. He was born in March. Traditionally March was always the first time in the calendar year that an Army unit would go into the bush to train. This was the case for me—I seemed to always be in the bush for his birthday.

To make a deadline, I was forced to organise my own Army exercise over my son's birthday. As the commander on the ground, I excused myself so I could take him to lunch and kick a ball with him in the park—the ball was a birthday present. Saying goodbye that day was like a bullet to the head. I realised I wanted more from my life; I needed more time with my kids. This was the very alarm bell I needed—there were more important things in life than my career. My kids would only be young once, and I was missing the best bits. I needed to formulate an exit strategy from the Army, but the same issue arose yet again. What would I do?

I decided that the best course of action for me was to remove myself from competing with my peers for promotion. I needed to set myself up at least geographically to be closer to the kids; I was missing so much of their young lives.

With Margie and I separating, she and the kids had moved back to the Gold Coast. I needed to be at least posted to Brisbane, where I could remain in the Army, earn a decent living, and do a job that I not only liked, but I was good at. I would just have no career prospects. I was happy with this decision—family first.

I was content that my career sacrifice to spend time with my kids would be worth it. I sought positions in Brisbane. I knew once and for all that I would be able to live a fulfilling personal and professional life: I still had a lot to offer the Army and I wanted to make sure I did this for as long as I could. I was posted into the Plans Team at the Army's Divisional Headquarters at Enoggera Barracks, the very place where all those years earlier, I was a candidate on the Army Officer Selection Board.

As a member of the Plans Team, I was responsible to the Australian Government for planning any humanitarian and disaster relief support within the Pacific. Part of this was the facilitation of a bi-annual activity in Papua New Guinea, assisting their defence force to plan for their own disaster relief contingencies.

While planning this activity it was suggested a day trip to the Kokoda Trail be investigated. I was keen, but where was the trail in relation to Port Moresby? I asked a friend who was planning with me to look into it.

The plan for the activity was set. We had a spare weekend in the middle of two weeks work. With this, we sought people to assist us walking a section of Kokoda.

My friend found a guy who ran Kokoda Treks. He was going to be in Port Moresby that weekend and was able to facilitate this for us. He would personally take us out for the day.

I found him to be a great guy, really personable—we had an amazing time on the trail, I loved it! It was muddy, it was hot, it was humid, and it was steep. It was everything I loved. I was in the bush, and I was on a section of one of Australia's most significant war sites. I don't recall the last time I smiled that much or had that much fun. I was in my element. I loved being on such a historical part of Australia's story. I knew that one day I would be back to do the trail in its entirety.

Standing at the top of Imita Ridge on the Kokoda Trail, my first taste of Kokoda. I knew I wanted to come back and complete the entire trek. Little did I know I would do it as a job - a new career direction was in the making.

It was that afternoon over a beer that our host asked if I wanted to walk it some more. Absolutely! He offered to take me back—he wanted to use me as a guide. I told him how I was thinking about discharging from the Army and that I was seeking the right thing to do. This was a very attractive option for me to consider part-time. With my initial thought of a possible transfer from the Regular to the Reserve Army, this would allow me to do two things that I loved part-time—this excited me. We decided to remain in contact.

The activity the following week was a great success. The morning we'd leave New Guinea, we woke to the news that a Malaysian aircraft had been shot out of the sky over the Ukraine. Over breakfast we made light-hearted jokes about not wanting to be one of the Russian Separatists we'd heard responsible. We had one day off prior to re-commencing work.

As I opened the door to the office that morning, there were people everywhere. My boss gave me a look which told me how relieved he was to see me, I was curious, I had no idea what all the activity was the cause of.

My boss walked straight towards me, telling me to go home and pack, he and I were flying to the Ukraine that night. He told me what he wanted me to prepare and asked, 'what else do we need to take?' I pointed across the desk at my colleague saying, 'we need him. We'll get there and realise we need more people, we'll make the request, and they'll arrive two weeks later—let's take him now'.

My boss agreed, telling both of us to go and prepare to depart that night. My colleague mouthed the words, 'I love you!' Laughingly, I said to him that out of the two of us, he was the better planner. If only one of us was going, it should be him. I respected him, he needed to be there—he is the best planner I'd seen in my career, far better than me.

7pm that night I was standing at Brisbane International Airport, heading to the Netherlands, via Dubai. I asked the boss when we'd be back; he was unsure, hoping before November—his pregnant wife was due to give birth that month.

The next month was to be one of the hardest and most rewarding months of my career. I saw highly tense situations, I saw friction between local and international forces, and I saw the necessity to be political, humanitarian, and direct—all in one setting.

Possibly one of the most difficult things was watching five nations—Dutch, Malaysian, Ukrainian, and the Russians, along with us—working in and around one another, trying to maintain the status quo.

Add to this, we had our Australian Federal Police in addition to the Dutch Police, so it wasn't all military that had to work together—there were friction points between civil and military forces from various nations. The positive to the friction points, we all wanted the best course of action, nobody wanted to stop the other from helping, the friction was more how we all worked together for the best outcome.

We needed to get people to the crash site, and we needed the deceased and artifacts returned to the Netherlands for forensic assessment. One of the first things they found when they arrived at the site was the area had been sanitised by the Ukrainians. They'd swept and cleaned it, placing the bodies and the wreckage onto a train, but for political reasons the Ukrainians wouldn't release the train to us. When it was released, it was transported to the north of the country, this meant we could repatriate everything to the Netherlands.

It's hard to see people in distress. On one of the days, an estimated one million people lined the streets, crying as the hearses carrying the slain passed by. Each casket was removed from an Australian Air Force plane, each with eight members of the Dutch defence force carrying it on their shoulders—slow marching to the awaiting hearse. I was in the operations room within the Dutch Ministry of Defence, watching this unfold on their large screen. I turned to see the crowd in this room all sobbing, we knew that we had the responsibility to get this one right. We went straight back to work and continued with some very long days.

I had days that were quiet, and I had days where our people (in this instance our military and Australian Federal Police) were being either shot at or over. When being shot over, it was either the Russians or the Ukrainians shooting at the other with our people in between.

One of my roles was the coordination of people in and out of several countries at once. This was in addition to the reporting required and assisting with the plan to get people back out again—that is having already planned to get them in. While it was intense, it was what was required, and I loved every minute of it.

This was vastly different to my work in Afghanistan, but I was on operations and doing my job for real once again. I knew in the back of my mind that this would be my last operational deployment, so I made the days count, embracing each one and accepting the challenges. I loved it.

At the completion of this job and my return from the Netherlands, I planned my extraction from the Regular Army. I contacted the Kokoda guy and together we put a plan in place for me to walk Kokoda with him the following April. Within this plan, I would work for him as a guide, while taking my long service leave from the Army. This would allow me to transition from the Regular to the Reserve Army, at the completion of my leave, with a discharge date from the Regular Army on 11 September 2015.

It's funny how much you become at peace with a massive decision like this when it's been done on your terms and the timing is right. The Army had changed me a lot, but with this decision I could feel the old Cam coming back, but it would still take time to 'de-Army' me back to my pre-Army days. Still, I was well on my way to achieving this, and for the first time in a long time, I was genuinely happy.

The following April I was once again back at the Brisbane International Airport, this time I was flying to Port Moresby to walk Kokoda. I was beyond excited! This would be the first thing I had done in so many years that wasn't related to the Army, but noting Kokoda is a military history tour, it still had a military flavour to it.

I had studied the Battle of Kokoda at Duntroon and had completed my own research, but now I would get to see it firsthand and be able to better make sense of my research. I was ready to get my teeth into it, from what I had seen nine months earlier on that day trip. I was psyching!

The day came and we were off. I started to see the difference between trekking with civilian hikers and trained soldiers—I liked this. It lacked the over-macho bull and had real people with real emotions—it was ok to be in distress. What I loved more than anything about this experience—more than the location, the culture, the history, or the remarkable story that went with it—was the leadership challenge!

Leading soldiers for the most part is quite easy, they've all been trained and inculcated with a set of values. Here I had a cross-section of the community with no two people trained the same. If it got bad, unlike in the Army, I wasn't allowed to yell at them or use a 'because I told you so' argument to reach my desired outcome. This was awesome!

We completed the trek, and I was asked what I thought. Did I want to do it as a Guide? 'Hell yes! I am so in!' said with a lot of enthusiasm. That was it then. I'd fly home to Brisbane and five days later, I'd fly back to start my first trek as a Guide. I was so happy; I was well on the way to being me again.

11 September 2015 came, and two things were happening that day. Firstly, I was on my final day in the Australian Regular Army and secondly, Dad was to attend a routine oncology appointment—as a family we knew this would be a big appointment. Lainie and I attended the appointment with Mum and Dad. I chose to be absent without leave on my final day in the Army to make sure I was there for the family—family first! I look back now and laugh that at no stage in my career did I do anything that I should have been charged with; but chose on my final day to break a military law. What would they do, charge me? It was a no-brainer.

Over the next 18 months I would cross Kokoda 10 times. I loved it, it was everything that I wanted, but as you can imagine, it's not the sort of thing that you can make a full-time wage out of. Besides, the very reason I wanted to leave the Army was to have more time with the kids, not replace the Army with another job that would have me away from home.

As much as I loved being away on my own terms and the feeling that I was living, exploring, and meeting amazing new people—showing and helping them achieve life goals, I decided it was time for me to leave the company. I resigned my position as a Guide, deciding to focus on working in the Army, albeit in a part-time capacity for now.

Several months passed and I was doing enough to keep busy—I kept thinking about Kokoda. I missed the place a lot more than I thought I would. I missed the people, I missed the culture, I missed the social side, and I missed the leadership that came from it. I longed for it.

At no stage did I consider working for another company, I don't know why, but I ran some basic numbers and believed I could start my own. What resonated with me was that I would be able to do it my way, give it my own personal spin a little more and dig a little deeper into the psychological side of warfare. I saw with my experience in combat situations, in both in the Afghanistan and Ukrainian campaigns, that I could create my own model, help those that came to trek understand with greater depth what the soldiers on Kokoda in 1942 would have felt—my own point of difference. There was one issue though—I didn't have the funds to start this company on my own. There was only one person I knew who had the money, the business knowledge, and the love to help me do this—Mum. I made a call and said I was coming to see her with a proposal.

The following day I drove to the Gold Coast to see Mum. I asked her what she thought of the idea and if she wanted to go into business with me, I would be doing all of the heavy lifting and she could help me with the day to day running of the business. I figured it would give her some inspiration for her days noting the passing of my father five days after that fateful appointment on my final day in the Regular Army. I knew she'd be helping me, and in time, she'd financially benefit. She was keen, but not to work, or mentor me and or do anything other than lend me the money required to set me on my way.

That was it then! I was off, into the dark hollow world of running a small business, with the cash and not one clue of what I had to do to make this work.

What I needed above all else was guidance. I needed an accountant—one that will understand my idea and is willing to go on this crazy ride with me. I attacked Google.

There were three advertisements that came up on my search of 'Business accountants Brisbane'. I looked at the second one, I loved their tag line, which was 'We're proud to be your boring accountants'. I looked at the one first in the list, it didn't grab me, I looked at the third one, same thing, nothing. I went back to the second one 'We're proud to be your boring accountants', I loved it. I made the call.

The first thing you get when you talk to Rob, the 'boring accountant' is that he is young enough to understand your crazy idea, and old enough to have the experience you want when you start your first business—he's active, and he's personable. We made an appointment to meet the following week at his office.

When we met, he was everything his voice had told me. Around 45, lean, fit, well dressed, casually in jeans and a t-shirt, shaved head and educated—I liked him immediately. He reached his hand out to shake mine and welcomed me, ushering me into an office and getting right to it. 'So, Cam, you want to start a company and you want to take people over the Kokoda Trail for a living—are you nuts!?' What I learnt in the first two minutes talking to Rob, was if this was going to work, he was my guy.

Having mapped everything out on a whiteboard, Rob told me the things that I needed to do, and the things that he would do and when we would meet again to make this official.

The first thing I needed to do was to see a lawyer to 'Trademark' my business names. He gave me the name of his lawyer and that was dealt with. Businesses were registered in both Australia and Papua New Guinea, licence applications were completed, then approved and then all I had to do was build a website and launch. Easy!

The day came, I was set ready to go, I had my website finished, I had my emails set up and I had created a Facebook page with one follower—me! I sat wondering if I should wait another few days, a week maybe. Was I going to do it? I can't, this is mental... filled with the greatest depths of self-doubt, I couldn't. Then I did it, without thinking I had hit 'publish' on my website, I was live. Next, I went onto my new business Facebook page and wrote 'Welcome to 100% Kokoda'. I went to my personal Facebook page, and wrote 'Team, I have started my own business, 100% Kokoda. If would like to come and see Kokoda, I want to take you, can I ask you to please like my 100% Kokoda Facebook page. Thank you for your support! Cam'.

I was live, I was the business owner of an Adventure Trekking Company that specialised in taking people across the Kokoda Trail in Papua New Guinea. What would happen? Time would tell, but I knew that I had a lot of work to do to be ready to actually take a trek.

Filled with self-doubt, I did it, I launched 100% Kokoda, hitting 'publish' on my website. I was live!

GETTING COMFORTABLE BEING UNCOMFORTABLE

'If it excites you and scares the shit out of you, that means you should probably do it.'

Jack Cheng

It's a funny thing when you work for yourself, the hours are the longest and the rewards are minimal. You have no income; you're working for the man—and you are 'the man'. The thing I was loving was that for all the hours, days, weeks, months, and years of my life that I'd dedicated to the Army, while I benefitted from the rewards of progressing a career, it really didn't equate to anything but a pay packet and some cool stories.

I learned quite quickly to love the time I was investing into my own business—I knew this would one day benefit me. I worked a lot of hours, to almost midnight every night, sitting on the lounge with my laptop drafting documents, writing safety briefs, safety support documentation for insurance policies, enquiring about public liability, business insurances, bank fees, company tax implications, Business Activity Statements; a lot of learning about a lot of things that up until this point, I knew nothing about. I also wrote to a lot of people, companies, businesses, sporting teams, telling them about my company and how I could help them achieve greater teamwork from completing Kokoda with me. In one day I posted over 150 letters.

I set myself the goal that I wanted to take 30 people across Kokoda in my first year; I would recruit this 30. I wanted to take 60 in my second year. I worked on the theory that I would recruit another 30 people and the remaining 30 would come from word-of-mouth recommendations, one for every person I took in year one.

I planned my first trek for March the following year. I offered it for a price that would cover the business' costs and at least allow me to learn all the things I didn't know about Kokoda from a business perspective. First, I needed to find local labour. I didn't want to use any of the people I'd worked with previously in New Guinea; this was my 'line in the sand'. I wanted a fresh start, I wanted any success to be my own doing, and I didn't want someone from a rival company believing I'd taken their people. I needed to go to Port Moresby and I needed to find someone to be my point of contact.

It was a coincidence that Lainie knew a man from Papua New Guinea. Her son went to school with his son in Sydney. This man was working in Sydney for the Papua New Guinea Government. He knew a lot of people and got me in touch with a man from Efogi, a village right in the middle of the track. I arranged my trip to Port Moresby to go and meet this man.

My first impressions of Stanley were that he was an educated man with enough respect in the community to be my 'Chief Porter', the man that would lead the team. He knew men from the village who'd previously worked as Porters, (the title afforded to the men who carry). None of these men were currently employed and none of them had ever worked for my old company; this was perfect. I discussed my vision for 100% Kokoda—he loved it. But in his village, he'd seen white men make promises before—I'd have to show him and the village through my actions that I meant what I'd said. I needed them to see that I'm a man of my word.

I travelled to Port Moresby on several more occasions to finalise various things, like storage for my equipment, hotels for accommodation, charter planes to fly between Kokoda and Port Moresby, and I tried to obtain a bank account. I also needed to locally buy many items that were required to be operational, things like machetes, cooking equipment, tarps, ropes etcetera. I purchased packs and tents in Australia and was, for all intents and purposes, ready. We just needed people to take, this is where I learnt the most lessons of all.

Social media and marketing can be fickle beasts. I spoke with friends who ran small businesses, learning from them. The main lesson I learnt was that it's a lot of trial and error—a lot of trialling with a lot of errors! The more errors I made, the closer I would be to understanding the people who would follow us, and I needed social media followers.

Having been a member of a family that ran small businesses, I knew you had to spend money to make money, I decided to run a competition on Facebook—a competition that asked people to 'like and share' my page to go into the draw to win a free trek to Kokoda.

My numbers increased, not rapidly, but enough. I drew the prize on Christmas Eve, I was thrilled when a lady whom I'd known for many years won it; she's a lovely woman and the best part for me at least, she's well connected! This wasn't rigged, it was just meant to be. By the end of January, I had five takers for my first trek, I knew four of them and the one I didn't know, was my nephew's friend. This was perfect, this would allow me to iron out the issues with people who understood this was our maiden voyage, that there would be some teething problems—they were mature and willing to allow me to do this.

9 March 2017 was the day that I'd waited for, this was no longer a drill, we were live, and we were about to set off on our first trek—we had an issue. My nephew Lachlan was unable to arrive the day before as is required—he had a funeral to attend. He would arrive at lunch time on the day of the trek's departure, not ideal but not horrific either.

We arrived at the airport early, hoping that Lachlan would be off the plane quickly, grab his bags, clear customs and we would be off. His plane landed, time passed, people came through the door, then nobody else. We waited and waited and waited. I called my sister back in Sydney, she reassured me that he'd departed that morning, when finally, Lachlan walked through the door of customs holding a plastic bag, he had no other bags.

Lachlan told us how his bag had not made the transfer through Brisbane from Sydney—we'd have to wait. 'Not going to happen' my thought, we had to go. I'd worked far too hard and waited far too long not to go right now. So, we saw the baggage clerk, provided him the phone number of my local contact, and told my contact that I'd pay for someone to catch up to us with the bag the following day when it arrived. It was a long shot and honestly, I held little to no faith the plan would work, but I was not failing on the first day of the first trek of my new business.

We drove out of Port Moresby, Lachlan with only the clothes that he was wearing, a water bottle, an apple, and a ham sandwich. That was all he had to start his Kokoda adventure.

It's an amazing feeling when you walk under the gates of the Kokoda Trail for the first time. Once you have had that feeling, you don't get it again, that's until you walk under them for the first time as the owner of a business. You have the lives of these people in your hands, their families are counting on you not to harm them, and you have the lives of the porters in your hands too—on this day, we had six porters in the team. Our maiden journey was 40 minutes old before we had to stop for the night—waiting for Lachlan at the airport had stolen the daylight we needed to make it any further, but that's ok, flexibility is a principle of war, we're here now. I took the satellite phone out of my pack to call home to let them know that we were safe for the night—nothing, the phone that was working perfectly fine this morning, is now giving me nothing, seriously! This can't be happening, how was it that my safety lifeline, that I have used, tried, and tested was now failing? I begin thinking, 'when it rains, it pours on Kokoda' and then it rained, and then it poured, quite literally. Life on Kokoda, it's never dull.

On night two, a miracle happened, a young guy came running up the hill to where we were staying, covered in sweat, carrying a pack—it was Lachlan's pack. This guy had run with a pack, the same distance that took us a day to walk, in just three hours. We thanked him, paid him, fed him, and gave him somewhere to rest. We were complete, the trek could now continue as I had planned.

We finished that first trek with a lot of lessons were learned by me, with no inkling to the Adventurers, which is always good. When the client doesn't realise that there has been an issue and it's resolved before they find out, this is always a good thing. I was content with knowing what I needed to do to make it better again—for one, larger groups not filled with people that I know!

By the end of the first year, I'd taken five treks and 37 people across the track—a successful year that hit my target. The local communities respected who we were and what we were trying to achieve. Rival trekking companies were taking note, with people who initially questioned my credibility, now very quiet. I was happily in 'my lane' which was to be a smaller company that offered the best treks I could provide; I wanted my Adventurers loving their experience and my desire was for them to be the happiest people on the track. One thing I saw a bit of and hated, was members of other companies questioning my clients, asking them why they'd chosen my company over theirs. It was arrogant to ask such a question.

My belief is that once a sale has been made and the client has booked with a company—mine or another—it's up to the other operators to no longer be attempting to sell that person their own trekking experience, they should be selling that person the destination. When I've discovered someone has purchased a trek from a competitor, I've told them how they will have the best time, giving credit to their decision on their chosen company, making them believe that this will be the most amazing experience, not creating negativity or doubt.

I don't know why you'd think by trying to discredit a competitor will make a client want to buy your product. To me it's insane! I would never think this if I was the client, which is the model I created, I wanted to be the business that I would want to buy from if I was a client—be it when a sale is made or the respect I am shown in the event I've chosen another provider.

I can't tell you the number of calls and emails that I have received from people asking me what boots they should be wearing on Kokoda, knowing perfectly well they weren't coming with me. I figured if I could help them to have a good time, that they will remember that I was helpful, and think we're good people. Often, these people would see me out there and come and say hello—is this not what it's all about? Sure, I want their business, but I want a good reputation more.

The second year, the model that I'd created was working, people were resonating with seeing Kokoda 'through the eyes of the soldiers'—my point of difference. My original goal of selling 60 treks in my second year was blown away—in nine treks we took 108 people across Kokoda. I was thrilled and knew that I had to try to maintain this momentum, against the first-world problem of growing too fast, too soon. There was only so much that I could do myself before the product quality declined, this was the last thing I wanted; this was why I had called the business 100% in the first place. I had to grow organically, at a rate that I could sustain.

The tricky part of business which I knew that I would have to deal with at some point was the challenge of needing staff while not being able to afford them.

What to do? Should I stay at the same level running all treks myself and not advance? Should I put my prices up so the demand dealt with the limited supply, and therefore risk losing a portion of my market by pricing myself out of it? With increased client numbers, should I take a hit in losing profitability by employing someone else to assist facilitating my treks? Hoping that if I did take on additional people, that they emotionally invested into the business with my values and met the standards I'd set—the very standards that created this demand in the first place.

I knew more people having a brilliant experience on my treks would generate even more word-of-mouth advertising. I knew that this would then bring even more business, but it was hard not being in total control. This was something that took some getting used to. I had to trust I'd recruited the right people to lead my treks. I had to trust they were leading them as I expected—maintaining my safety standards. I had to become comfortable that while the treks were being led differently to how I led them, I had to trust that the standard would be the same.

I was stressed, but happy—happy as there aren't too many businesses having this concern at the end of their second year of operation—many are closing their doors. I liked this problem.

The bad thing that happened in 2018 was I had a horrific year of health. For starters, I contracted malaria on the May Trek. While the risk of malaria to clients is minimal, to me as a trek operator it was far greater.

A lot of people think I'm crazy not to take a prophylaxis to prevent malaria—this is why I don't. I am fair skinned, and Doxycycline makes your skin sensitive to the sun. As a result, I get sunburnt a lot more than I usually would, and this leads to greater skin cancer concerns, which at 46 years old, I've already had my share. Sure, I use sun protection, but in a sweaty jungle, it only lasts so long and there are only so many times you can re-apply.

The drugs Malarone and Mefloquine make me quite sick. Lariam over a long duration affects the kidneys, and what a lot of people don't understand is that it's necessary to take most of these medications for up to four weeks on the completion of your journey. In my situation, I would be back in New Guinea and back on yet another cycle of medication before the previous cycle was complete.

Another matter is that a lot of these drugs don't actually prevent malaria, they stop the effects of it until you come off them. So by the time the effects are felt, you're at home where first-world medical treatment is readily available. Noting that I'm on Kokoda a minimum nine months of the year, I would therefore be on this medication for at least 10 months of every year. This is un-sustainable.

What I do however is sleep in a tent that has mosquito protection. I wear long sleeves and trousers at night, and I wear repellent. I was just bitten by the wrong mosquito. I think I know when it happened too. I had to make a call and got out of my tent to do so; it was at this point that I recall a mosquito getting me.

The recovery from malaria was terrible, walking to the mailbox required me to have to take a rest. I had no energy and I had zero stamina, but I knew that I had to get back to Kokoda; financially I couldn't afford to have other people leading that many treks for me, I needed to do some myself—if I didn't, it would bankrupt me. I needed to get back.

Two months later, I was feeling well enough and convinced the family that I would be ok, so I headed back to Kokoda and led my first trek since malaria. It wasn't pretty, but I took it slowly and walked with the group, not through the group like I normally would. I was back where I wanted and needed to be—we had a great trek. At the completion of this trek, I was filled with excitement, I knew when I returned for the next trek, my son Drew would come back with me to do his first Kokoda and I would get to take him on his first overseas adventure. I was bursting with excitement.

Standing proudly with Drew at the gates that signify the start of the Kokoda Trail. While I was smiling, I knew that my health wasn't good.

WHAT DOESN'T KILL YOU MAKES YOU STRONGER

Friedrich Nietzsche's adage that 'what does not kill me makes me stronger' may be true, what it fails to associate is that it almost kills you.

Cam James

The next trek came around quickly, Drew and I were ready. We were leaving Brisbane and headed to Port Moresby. Drew was excited to be travelling overseas for the first time and I was excited to be sharing this adventure with him.

On our second day, as per my normal pre-trek routine, we headed off to the shops to buy the food required for the trek. Drew was blown away by the city and its poverty. This was an exciting day for Drew and rightly so; he quickly noticed that everywhere he walked, he had at least two of my guys following him; he had his own personal security detail.

That night we had dinner at the hotel, we sat reminiscing on the day. Drew said how lucky he felt compared to the people he'd seen that day, a great sign for me as it was one of the main reasons I wanted him to come. In the months leading into this moment, he was starting to get a little 'entitled', I wanted him to see how other people lived. I needed him to get some perspective on his own life and the benefits that came from living in a first-world, middle-class society.

The dinner service at the hotel can be ridiculously slow, and being tired, we wanted to eat and leave so that we could get back to our room and rest. I decided to order one of their pizzas, they're normally good, and usually come pretty fast. But on this night, the pizza that I ate was anything but good, the base felt undercooked, and it just didn't taste quite right. I'd only eaten a portion of it before I decided I'd had enough.

Finishing dinner we headed back to our room to lie in our beds and watch a movie, for now, everything was normal. I was happy, I had my boy, and with the arrival of the clients tomorrow, we were both excited for the day and the coming week ahead. Then it happened.

I started to feel a sharp pain in my abdomen, was it my stomach? My pizza choice now seemed like a terrible decision. I kept thinking that I should have had something different for dinner, the pains exponentially starting to increase. I looked across to Drew who had fallen asleep, typically well before the end of the movie. I cursed this kid's ability to fall asleep so quickly.

As I lay awake all night in the most excruciating pain I'd endured to date, I cursed my son's ability to sleep through anything. I tossed and turned all night, vomiting time and time again. I was sick to the point that I had nothing left in my stomach to vomit.

My now empty stomach and my abdomen were feeling rock hard from the contracting convulsions they'd now endured for several hours. I decided to lay on the cool tiles of the bathroom, with nothing but that disgusting 'bile' feeling burning my throat and filling my mouth. I couldn't stay here, so I got up, cleaned my teeth once again, as I'd done so many times that night—thinking that all the noise I'd been making would surely wake Drew. He slept through it all.

At daybreak I woke Drew, explaining to him that I'd been sick all night, very sick—something was wrong with me, and I needed to go to the hospital. I'm normally not a big fan of taking pain relief, but I knew I needed to get something to help, the pain that I was experiencing was too much for

Panadol and Nurofen. Abnormally for me, I had tried taking it and it had done absolutely nothing at all to help my dire situation.

I explained to Drew that the only available opportunity for me to go to the hospital was before the clients arrived; how once they'd arrived, we'd have no time—we'd have to entertain them, and we'd have work to complete to be ready to leave the following morning. I asked Drew if he wanted to come with me or if he wanted to stay at the hotel for breakfast and a swim. This seemed like a good choice, but he was having no part of it—he was coming with me.

We walked into the hotel lobby to see Charlie, the hotel bus driver, whom I knew quite well, asking him if he was able to take us to the hospital. There was a benefit to being such a good customer to this hotel, one that brings them a lot of business (especially in the bar sales before and after treks), so of course they'd accommodate this small request.

We also knew Charlie had the time to take us, it was still hours before check-out and even more time until he needed to do his daily runs to drop off and collect new guests from the airport. He explained there was a choice of hospitals—the choices were: the Port Moresby Public Hospital or the Pacific International Hospital, the private one—no brainer. I'm in a third-world country, I have private health insurance, there was no decision to be made, take me to the private one. We made the short drive to the hospital and even sitting in the hotel bus I was uncomfortable—the pain, while less now than it was in the early hours of the morning, was still bad enough. I was just so uncomfortable, I couldn't sit still, every different way I tried to sit was painful and every minor bump in that third-world road was jolting through me.

We arrived at the hospital, I informed Charlie, that I'd call him when I needed him to come back to collect us. In his thick Tok-Pisin accent, he says 'ok'. Drew and I walked into the emergency department to the inquisitive stares from the crowd of locals who were looking at the only two white faces in the room. There was a long line of people waiting to speak to the receptionist. We were asked to bypass them and go to the front of the queue—we refused. The lady in front of us thanked us for not thinking we were better or more important than they were. We knew we weren't; it was up to us to wait our turn—we were after all visitors in their country.

My turn to talk to the receptionist came and I explained my situation. I was led to another part of the emergency department, where they did the usual, name, age, blood pressure, temperature checks etcetera. I was offered a bed in the triage room.

The doctor wanted to run some basic blood tests to assess the cause of my pain. Before they started however, I sent Drew to the café to go and get himself some breakfast. This would be the first of many visits for my son to this café.

The result of my blood test came back, they told me that I had food poisoning. This seemed logical, after all the pizza I ate last night tasted a little off, but I was a little more than curious how this was assessed from a blood test? To me a blood test would reveal more serious things and from what I learnt from having contracted malaria, it would allow them to assess the function of my liver, kidneys, but food poisoning? I wasn't so sure—but not being in the medical profession, I ran with it.

The doctor arranged for a nurse to attach a bag of antibiotics to me, offering me some pain medication. Noting how sick I felt earlier against how well I was feeling at that moment, I was happy to take them. I didn't want to be feeling that sick again, the medication seemed like a good idea. I was given enough to get me through the next two days. From what I knew about food poisoning, this would be sufficient.

An hour later I was given clearance to leave the hospital with a bag of pain medication. I had to get straight to the airport to meet the trekkers; the time taken at the hospital meant I now didn't have time to go back to the hotel to change into my 100% uniform, I had to go in the clothes I was wearing.

Having collected the clients, we took them to the hotel to get settled and briefed in for their adventure. All I knew was that the clients were happy, my son was happy, and I was in only a small amount of discomfort, so I was happy too. Everything seemed to be back on track.

When starting Kokoda for the first time, it's not uncommon for people to worry for a range of reasons. I have seen people question their training, concerned that they won't be able to keep pace with the group, or they are stressed about all the little things that to them remain unknown. Personally, I am rarely worried, but on this occasion, I was hoping that the discomfort I'd been experiencing would soon pass. It wouldn't.

That first day on Kokoda I could tell that something wasn't quite right; food poisoning should be passing by now. While the medication was working, it was only alleviating the pain for short periods—when the pain came back, it seemed worse every time. Every four hours I would take more medication and three hours after that I would be doubled over in pain once again.

Thanks to having malaria, I now knew what an inflamed liver felt like, I could feel mine—something wasn't right. But here I was on the Kokoda Trail, in the village of Kokoda, smiling to have a photo with my son under the arches that denote the start point. I was happy—unwell, but happy.

As we walked towards our camp, I felt increasingly unwell. Normally I can stroll the first section of the trail and maintain pace with the leaders, but on this day, I was with the back markers—struggling.

Arriving at our night camp, I got the trekkers set up, fed and settled for the night.

I did my usual thing of checking on the porters, making sure that they had everything they needed, and that they knew the plan for the morning. They were eating their dinner and telling their stories, so I left them to it and headed to bed.

I would have been in bed for no more than ten minutes when the pain in my abdomen came back, hard! Already not well and in a considerable amount of pain, I was now back in the land of exponential increases in pain and discomfort. The problem was, I was now over a 100-kilometre walk and

6000 metres of elevation away from the nearest facility that could help. I was isolated and all I had to keep me company was the pain that would keep me awake all night. I was now out of pain medication, and not only was the pain not going away, if anything, it was getting worse!

Have you ever had a night when every micro-movement in your body was painful? Well, that was the night that I was having, I did not sleep at all. My abdomen was like a taut balloon, blown up as hard as it could be without popping. It felt like it would explode at any moment. As much as I tried to remain quiet, Drew, who was in the tent next to mine could hear me—he didn't get too much sleep that night either. We would wait and see what the new day would bring, hoping as is sometimes the case, that daylight makes the pain dissipate—it didn't.

As the first morning light struck the horizon, we woke the Adventurers for the day ahead. As is usually the case on the first morning of a trek, they took their time learning how to pack up, often putting things in and out of their packs a few times. We fed them their first breakfast and gave them time to fill water bottles, go to the bathroom, clean up and prepare—the porters ready for the day ahead had started to gather. While the clients had already started their journey, this was to be another morning of trepidation, the commencement of their first full day on Kokoda.

This day in this direction always has a slow start. It begins with a long walk up a gentle incline through the vast choko fruit vines that litter the area. I recall telling the Adventurers to leave, including Drew, I wanted to make my own way to the top. This is something I always do; I normally catch them quite quickly. On this day however, like yesterday, I felt empty and with zero energy, clearly the result of a lack of sleep and food for concurrent days.

As we walked through the vines, Gary, one of the porters, came to me, he wanted to take my pack from me, 'It's not happening Gary'. The soldier in me refused to hand off my pack, I would never. He insisted, I felt too weak to argue, and reluctantly agreed.

It can take a lot to admit you're wrong, but Gary was right. I started to make better but still not great time, catching the Adventurers at the bottom of the final steep climb before reaching the village of Isurava.

Having caught the group at the rest point, I stopped short to empty my bladder, bright red blood urine gushed from me for now the second straight day. Something was severely wrong. The additional water consumed in hope it would pass was now only making it worse. I knew I was at a critical point, a decision had to be made, it needed to be a tough decision. I pressed on and pushed making this decision to the corner of my mind, it would have to wait, I had a job to do—mission first above all else.

Over the next ten minutes I went through the thought of all the planning I'd done to prepare to launch the business almost two years ago. With any good military planner, you always plan for the most likely thing that will happen, but you need to always consider and plan for the most dangerous thing that could happen too. I was now walking into my most dangerous course of action, which is as a guide, having to evacuate myself and leave the Adventurers in the trusty hands of the local labour—but the clients had all paid money for me to lead them.

While my company is not one of these, there are companies who sell treks led by the locals. These treks traditionally sell $1000 cheaper per person than a trek with an Australian guide. This is what I would have to do in my most dangerous situation, so the decision was made that if I had to leave, I would offer them each a $1000 refund—as an act of goodwill. I didn't want them feeling that I'd taken advantage of a situation and benefitted— still, I pressed on.

Strange things run through your mind at a time like this. While I was still in 'game mode', part of me knew that my day was done and I would soon be back in that hospital, the one that gave me no confidence with the food poisoning diagnosis. I thought of my mum's saying that 'everything happens for a reason'. I wondered what the reason could be for me to be this sick, right here, helpless, and exposed, this far into the trail—why now?

Then it hit me; Drew being with me was the reason! Why was it, that he was here with me right now on this trek, the first time that I am really, and I mean really unwell, out here and this isolated. I paused and looked at him and said to him 'you're the reason'. He looked confused and rightly so, he'd not just spent the last three hours in my head. I called out to the Adventurers and asked them to come over; I needed to talk to them.

I explained that I was unwell, they knew that. I looked at my son and said to the group 'had you have come with a company on a 'locally led' trek, it would have been $1000 cheaper per-person than coming with me. This is my most dangerous situation'. Looking at my son, it made me realise that he needed me as a father a lot more than they needed me as a guide. I apologised that I needed to evacuate myself to make sure that I lived for my kids. They understood the gravity of the situation and agreed that my leaving was the right decision. I was gutted. I hated letting them down, but at that moment I honestly believed it was the right thing, I was the weakest member of the team. I was struggling and wanted them to have the best experience, had I stayed, I risked compromising their adventure.

I took the satellite phone from my pack and made a call to the office in Australia. This was standard procedure when we intend to evacuate someone. I wanted Katrina in the office near her phone, positioned for the details and ready to call insurance and helicopter companies. I told her that I needed to execute an evacuation, and as per our procedures, she asked who? 'Me!' There was silence on the other end of the phone.

I explained that I was sick and that I would call her back when I got to Isurava village, but to action the casualty evacuation plan for me, from Isurava village; I would be there in an hour.

It's a horrible feeling watching your team leave without you. If I could give you an example to ponder, I would imagine the feeling I encountered at that point would be like falling overboard from a ship and watching it moving away from you, leaving you stranded. In this instance however, I had the means to call for help, I still had the satellite phone to call for updates on my evacuation. I would give the phone to the porters who remained with me as their means to call for emergency assistance once I'd departed.

Noting my necessity to keep the phone, this was my most vulnerable time, not as a patient, but as a business operator. I had a real concern that one of the trekkers would injure themselves while separated from the phone, and there would be no means for the team to communicate with the outside world. However, an injury to one of them was a possibility—I was a probability, so it was more important that I had it for now—I just wanted the helicopter to come and collect me. The sooner the helicopter came, the sooner I could hand the satellite phone to the boys and the less vulnerable the team would be.

I called again, I needed an update on the helicopter, it should be arriving at any moment. The reality of my situation became even more serious.

Between my calls with Katrina, she'd contacted my travel insurer, they'd informed her that I had no insurance—I wasn't covered. There was nothing they could do to help me, more to the point, they wouldn't do anything to help me.

How could this be? 'I buy an annual policy at the start of every trekking season; this always includes helicopter evacuation for a medical emergency—there is no way I'm not insured'.

While operating as 100% Kokoda, we'd evacuated several injured trekkers who were each incapable of continuing—this wasn't a new process for us. We're anally retentive with safety and insurances, I knew I had my own; I remembered buying the policy only months prior.

It turned out that when I ordered my insurance over the phone, the consultant had sold me a 12-month policy for one trip, not the 12-month policy that allowed for the unlimited trips as I'd requested! This meant they weren't coming to get me—I was left vulnerable, isolated, and literally laying in the dirt. I kept wondering who in their right mind would think I wanted to buy a 12-month insurance policy for a single, two-week trip? It made no sense.

Pondering this was helping nobody. I was still in the middle of the New Guinea jungle, gravely ill, my son with me and requiring an immediate evacuation. I desperately needed medical assistance. There's a lot going through your mind at a time like this.

Katrina was now on the phone to not only the insurer, but also to the local charter companies we use—they would see what they could do to assist me. The likely asset that could come had been seconded by a mining company; it was currently on task and would not be able to arrive for at least another 24-hours. My most dangerous situation had now, somehow, become even more dangerous.

The decision was made; as I was incapable of moving, I would stay where I was, with Drew and three of the porters who would have to catch up to the group the following day. I was now laying on a slight grassy incline, the incline helped to take the pressure off my abdomen. The porters started setting up tents nearby, allowing me to rest between phone calls. The porters were amazing—they took care of Drew, they made us dinner and while I tried to eat, I couldn't think about food, I was too sick. With the sun still well up, I went to bed; I needed to sleep.

I watched the roofs of the houses begin to lift and flap under the cyclonic like winds coming from the rotor wash. I started thinking 'oh here we go, t his will happen now, the roofs will fly off and I will be responsible for re-building all of the houses in the village!'

At some point in the early evening, I needed to go to the bathroom; the pain encompassing my body while moving was intolerable. Drew hearing my groans looked worried as did Porters, Gary and Joseph, who ran to assist me walking to the toilet. It took three minutes with a porter under each arm to negotiate a 30-metre walk.

After another restless night of little to no sleep, I woke to a message on the satellite phone that I needed to be ready at 8am for the helicopter. We packed and waited—the helicopter arrived right on time.

There's always excitement when a helicopter arrives in one of the villages, today was to be no different. With me stumbling towards the landing site with a porter supporting me under each shoulder, crowds of villagers had come to watch the excitement, running around all yelling at each other in one of their three languages—Tok Pisin, English and the local dialect of Koiari. Some of the villagers seemed somewhat concerned and curious about what could be wrong with me.

As the helicopter descended, I watched the roofs of the houses begin to lift and flap under the cyclonic like winds coming from the rotor wash. I started thinking 'oh here we go, this will happen now, the roofs will fly off and I will be responsible for re-building all of the houses in the village!' But to my relief, under the intensity of the rotor wash, thankfully they held.

Drew and I were ushered to the door of the helicopter by the pilot, helmets placed on, and seat belts fastened. Gary waved. Moments prior he had given me a hug and told me to get better. I assured him that I would be ok. I don't know if it was blind belief, hope, or if I believed it, but my journey back to health hadn't even begun.

Much like when I had malaria, I was of the belief that I would get to hospital, they would make me better, and I would bounce back in a few weeks. How wrong I was.

I looked at my son sitting in the helicopter, he was nervously excited waiting for us to take off. The doors close, the pilot looked back and asked if we were ok? I was happy that I was getting out of there and would soon be receiving medical treatment. Katrina had made plans to come and take care of Drew, it was likely I would be in hospital for a few days, and I was in no fit state to care for him in a foreign country.

The pilot spoke over his radio and with that, we were airborne. As we looked out of the windows, we were already high above the village, the crowds of people on the ground all looking up at us. I could see the boys looking and waving, and then we were gone, next stop, Port Moresby, albeit through the dangerous flight line of Papua New Guinea's Yodda Valley.

As we approached Port Moresby, I arranged for Charlie to take us to the hospital. Noting that many people in this part of the world are on pre-paid phones and almost never have credit, it wasn't unusual for me not to get a reply from him. To my joy, within five minutes of being on the ground he arrived, with a smile—confused, but happy to see me.

I thanked the pilot and the office for their assistance. They mention an invoice requiring payment—I was confused. They informed me that Katrina had said that she, and not the insurance company would pay for the airframe. Too sick to debate, I went with it. I was of the belief that in the interest of expediting this process that she must have organised to pay for the airframe, and the insurance company would be reimbursing me later.

I informed them she was flying into the country that afternoon, I would arrange for her to come and pay. They seemed happy. I gave them a business card, so they at least had my details, and I got out of there. I needed the hospital and I needed it badly.

Bypassing the queue at reception, I went directly to the emergency department, walking in to see the same doctor who had treated me for 'food poisoning' just days prior. He looked confused and pointed me to the same bed I'd occupied last time.

Laying down he could clearly see how much discomfort I was in. He asked me again what the problem was, and I described in detail the things I'd encountered. While the pain still hadn't passed, the pain medication he'd given me last time seemed to work, above all else, I wanted something as soon as practicable to alleviate the pain.

The doctor called for the same nurse—she had left me with little confidence on my last visit—she was to take bloods. They wanted to assess a new sample to see what they could discover. Like my last visit, they hooked me up to an intravenous drip and once again began feeding antibiotics into me, but this time they also arranged for pain medication, which arrived in a small clear cup being held by a woman carrying an EFTPOS machine.

The lady with the drugs and the EFTPOS machine informed me that I had to pay for everything as I went. I asked her if we could create an account and pay one transaction when I discharged, whenever that may be. I didn't want to pay for the international penalty my bank charges per credit card transaction when overseas. This penalty equates to $12 AUD, per transaction. My request was denied! Frustrated once again with PNG logic, or the lack thereof.

The doctor returned as Drew was headed to the café; he'd been up for hours and was hungry. For the first time in days, I was feeling as though I could eat something, but I was thirsty, craving a juice. The doctor informed me there were irregularities with my results, he was waiting to liaise with his supervisor before deciding on a treatment. Additional information was required from both a urine and a stool sample.

Drew arrived with a chicken burger, and an orange and mango juice box for me—it was delicious! The flavour of the juice was soft and mellow, and I could taste the sweetness—I loved it, I could've destroyed a dozen more. Drew offered me some of his burger, I took a small bite, that too was delicious, I even pondered getting my own, but I knew one bite of his was enough.

As my boy and I laughed at the situation, the doctor re-appeared advising me that his supervisor wanted a feeding tube inserted. From the bloods, he was sure there was an issue with my intestinal function. Who was I to argue? This seemed right.

Just as Drew finished his burger, the doctor arrived with a small steel table on wheels, an array of items upon it. He sanitised his hands, placed gloves on and began to prepare. He opened a bag containing a clear tube and placed some type of lubrication on the end. He asked me to look towards the ceiling, advising that this may 'scratch' the back of my throat.

Now I have had a lot of uncomfortable moments in my life, just months earlier with malaria I had a catheter inserted, this was something I'd always feared. I now know that the fear of a catheter was misplaced; I should have feared nose tubes.

The doctor held my chin in his hand, my eyes firmly on the ceiling, when I felt the hose start its journey up my nose. I felt it pass behind my eyes as it began to make its journey downwards. It was at this point that I felt it pass my throat, my natural gag reaction as the tube scratched my throat. I coughed and gagged as he continued to push more of the tube in, stopping as I sat with my eyes filled with water and gagging. I looked at Drew, who was dry retching and looking like he was going to be sick from watching this procedure.

The doctor stated that as I had vomited, I was to be 'nil-by-mouth'. 'What!? I didn't vomit; I was choking on the tube that just 'scratched' its way past my throat!' I didn't really care about being nil-by-mouth—I was too traumatised. I can now hand-on-heart say, it was a million times worse than a catheter.

Time passed; and Katrina arrived taking in the sight of me laying there, still in my trekking clothes, now with a nose tube and looking worse for wear. She told us about her morning, I asked about the helicopter.

She began explaining how the insurance company remained indecisive about the payment, she knew she needed to get me out of the jungle, so she paid $4,000USD for my evacuation. For now, this was the least of my issues. I had a nose tube and had just paid for the privilege, complete with another $12 penalty fee.

The doctor returned once again, this time with his supervisor, explaining they believed I had a blockage in my intestines, they wanted scans to confirm. The issue, their CT was broken, they needed to do an ultrasound and an x-ray to see what they could discover.

Taken to a room, I was scanned prior to being returned to my curtained cubicle in the emergency ward. Upon my return, I paid for the scans, including, you guessed it, yet another penalty fee.

I was comfortable that they were working as hard as they could to ascertain the issue, but I was frustrated, which only grew when I was informed, they needed the bed I was in—I had to move to the ward. I was given options, with of course as you guessed, the payment details for each.

The options I was offered were for a single room at this rate, or a shared room at that rate. Noting I had just paid $4,000USD for a helicopter and knowing the financial position of the business, I couldn't afford to pay for a single room. Well, I could, but I couldn't justify it when I could share a room and pay half the fee—I chose the shared room.

It was a normal hospital room, a bathroom with a shower for four people, curtains drawn and my curtained room against the outside wall, so I had a window.

Drew returned from the café yet again; he decided the chicken burger was so good that he got himself another. Knowing I'd raved about the juice, he got himself one of them too. I took one look at the juice and snatched it from him—I was too thirsty not to have a crack at it. I didn't care that they said that I was nil-by-mouth, it was juice time! I took a sip and that heavenly nectar slid down my scratched throat once again; this time it was even better. But this time, two seconds after I drank it, we watched it come out of the tube in my nose into the collection bag attached to the bed. Drew and I laughed, Katrina was less than impressed, she's a stickler for the rules and nil-by-mouth means nothing! I was only allowed to suck the ice cubes I'd been given.

It was hot, and I stunk—I needed a shower and I wanted to cool down. I asked Katrina to open the window, it looked like there was a breeze outside. She opened the window just a little, the air flow passing over me was instantly cooling. If I couldn't eat, I would at least be comfortable.

My two doctors returned to give me the news of my scan. I had a blocked bowel, but they wanted to complete even more tests. I didn't know how they thought they were going to fix this. There was talk of surgery and an option of continued antibiotics to clear an infection which was caused by the blockage. Noting I'd been wheeled past the surgery to get to the ultrasound room, I knew I would not allow them to open my body in that room; it appeared to be no more sterile than a garden shed.

Over the course of the next two days, I was frequently seen by physicians; there was a lot of confusion as to what was now the cause of my condition. They no longer believed I had a blockage—they were speculating. Doctors came and went, providing 'updates' that didn't offer solutions—the one thing we knew, was that my health wasn't improving, if anything it was declining. I had bloods taken several times a day and the EFTPOS machine would rear its head every time. I'd begun wheezing uncontrollably with every breath, I was put on a ventilator, which if anything, made the wheezing worse.

Although my family members back in Australia were kept informed of my condition, they were left wondering what was going on. To be honest, even those of us inside the fog of the situation had no better idea, and we were the ones talking with the physicians!

A decision had to be made and it had to be made soon. If not made soon, we knew there was a genuine possibility that my return home would be in a casket or a bag, not in a seat or on a gurney.

I wanted to discharge myself from this hospital, I wanted to fly home to an Australian hospital, with real scans where we could appropriately deal with my issue. I needed the correct treatment to fix whatever was wrong with me—we still had no clarity to the actual issue.

Then for the first time I received some actual guidance about one of my conditions, the wheezing was pneumonia—I'd acquired it in this hospital. This hospital was now making me sicker, if I didn't leave, I knew I would die here. Having pneumonia meant that I was now unable to fly home commercially.

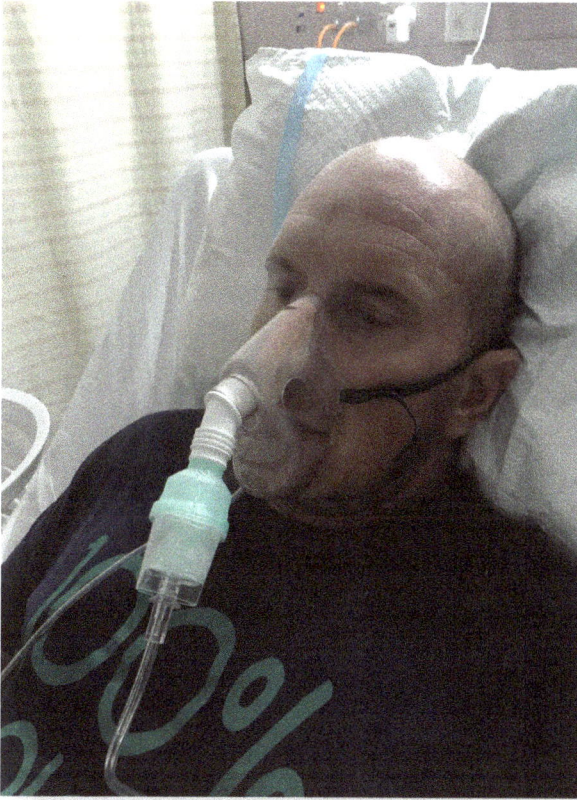

I honestly believed I would die in this hospital.

For the first time I received some actual guidance to one of my conditions, the wheezing, it was pneumonia—acquired in this hospital. This hospital was making me sicker if I didn't leave.

Having lost the ability to travel on a commercial flight, Lainie started investigating private medical evacuations—this was going to hurt financially. I no longer cared about money. I recall thinking that paying this off for the rest of my life and having a life longer than just today was now more important than any cost involved.

When Katrina and Drew arrived the following morning, I told them how overnight I sat up and watched a gunfight through the window. I had woken hot and opened the window to hear a commotion outside in the car park. Over the course of a minute or so, this disagreement escalated to the point that weapons were drawn, and shooting began. I laughed at the time at how typically PNG this was; I found humour in the fact that it happened in the carpark of a hospital. Regardless, this was yet another reason to get out of here.

I asked Katrina about the plan to get me out; we were still waiting on information from charter companies. I knew I needed to go, but part of me wanted to see if I could recover from the pneumonia just enough to allow me to fly home commercially. The cost of a private evacuation was a major concern. I questioned if I was able to tough it out for three hours on a commercial flight to Brisbane, and how it would be worth those hours of severe discomfort to not have to deal with the financial burden—it was money that I just didn't have.

Then it happened! I sat on the edge of the bed with a two-line cannula in my left arm. The lines were attached to a pole that held three IV bags: the third bag currently unused. A nurse walked in carrying protective gloves. Placing a glove on her right hand and putting the left glove into her tunic pocket, she began tracing the lines from the pole to the cannula—she wanted to use the third bag, the one that wasn't yet attached; but, to do this she needed to remove one of the bags attached to the cannula.

Over the next minute I watched her look of complete confusion—she had absolutely no idea and couldn't work it out. She then looked at the two lines into the cannula, one clearly open and the other closed. Detaching the line at the cannula that was currently closed, she then turned the dial to open it—before I could say 'stop!' the vein that for a few days now has had fluid being fed into it reacted by spurting blood back out through the opening. Instead of closing the dial on the cannula to stem the bleeding, she chose to place her hand over it, not her right hand with the glove, the unsterilised, un-gloved left hand!

I looked at Katrina with complete horror and said, 'I get out of here today, no matter what, I am going home!' I was done, I no longer cared what the hospital staff said or thought, I had lost all confidence in their ability to bring me back to health. I now believed there was a race to see what would kill me first. The race between whatever it was making me sick, and the staff—the race was neck and neck. I said to Katrina, 'I don't give a shit what it costs, make it happen, I'll make the call myself!' She took the hint, having seen this series of events; she too knew my survival depended upon it.

You know things are bad when your mother openly states and I quote, 'we need to get his body home, let's bring it home while it's warm'. The family was now very aware that death for me was now not only possible, it was imminent.

Lainie called a company from Brisbane, they could be there that afternoon and fly me home for treatment. The company went on to say that if they assessed that I was too sick, they would fly me straight to Cairns, a 30 to 40-minute flight. That was it, I started packing.

Even though I had started to pack, I knew I would have to wait. I had to wait for the plane to leave Australia, I would also need to be driven to the airport with clearance through customs, not the traditional way—I would be in an ambulance on the tarmac. I showered, packed, and sat ready and waiting in a wheelchair, still attached to the IV lines through the cannula.

Time stood still; at around 3pm I was told that the plane had taken off and I could make my way to the airport. I was placed onto a trolley, the lines taken off and the cannula for now remained in. I told Katrina to book flights for herself and Drew. Drew would have to come home by himself though, Katrina had to remain until the completion of the trek that was still underway. I needed her to welcome the Adventurers off the track and facilitate the required logistics. I also needed to finalise the payment of the accounts the hospital was still yet to bill—more penalty charges and a lot of things on an account that made no logical sense. I handed it to Katrina and asked her to do it, I didn't have the patience right now.

I was wheeled to a waiting room at the back of the emergency department, the very one that I'd walked into just days prior to begin this nightmare. I looked at the doctor who'd inserted the nose tube.

Hating him already, my hate turned to absolute rage, when he said, 'I'm glad you're going, we have no idea what's wrong with you'. My decision to leave at any financial cost had just been validated.

I was placed into an ambulance, a blood pressure machine attached to my right arm. I looked at Katrina and Drew who were standing together as the doors to the back of the Ambulance were closed. I saw them wave through the darkened windows—as we drove away, I literally wondered if I would ever see them again, believing I was close to the end. I could see the strain on both their faces. Drew, while clearly worried, didn't quite appreciate the gravity of the situation as much as Katrina.

Honestly, I just didn't want to die while in the care of anyone in PNG. If I died on the plane, I knew that Australians would do absolutely anything they could to save me, not like it was here where they appeared content not knowing what the actual problem was.

As the ambulance turned onto the main road at the front of the hospital, for some reason the driver turned on the siren and floored it! He took off so fast that the gurney I was on shot out of its locking mechanism, hitting the back door of the ambulance with such force that the doors burst open.

Fortunately, the attendant next to me, who like a 'henchman' on an 'Austin Powers' movie and pretending to be monitoring my condition on the 'machine that goes ping', was fast enough to lunge behind himself and with one arm grab the end of trolley, preventing me from flying out of the back of the ambulance and hurtling down the road amongst the traffic. I shook my head, thanked him, but thought once again, 'typical PNG'. That was at least the tenth time this week I'd had this thought.

We arrived at the airport with no other incident. I remained laying on the stretcher, desperately waiting to hear the news that the plane had landed—I was informed it was at least another 15 minutes away. I began adding the time in my head for the plane to land, taxi, park, do a handover. I knew that I would be here for at least another 45 minutes. I was so frustrated, but I knew that each minute spent had me one minute closer—it was a welcome relief.

The guy sitting next to me—the henchman, was talking to me, he was a nice enough man. He took my passport on my behalf to customs; this had me one step closer to getting out of here.

The plane landed literally 15 minutes after being told it would. I recall the feeling of pure joy running through me—I couldn't wait to be out of this ambulance. Five minutes after that, the guy next to me informed me that the plane had parked, the crew were disembarking; I began getting emotional just thinking about it—then I hear a familiar accent.

I couldn't see him, but the voice said to me through the door, 'we're here for you mate, I am just going to pee, I will be back to get you shortly'. Tears flowed; I couldn't help but burst into tears—the absolute joy of knowing I would be ok. This plane had cost my family $40,000 AUD, it was worth every cent. It would soon prove to be worth so much more than a monetary cost.

The same crew member returned a matter of minutes later, asking me how I was. I was so happy; he could clearly see the relief on my face. He advised me of his requirement to complete a handover, and how once completed he was going to help me to the plane. He asked me if I was right to walk, no matter how far away it was, I was good to go!

Having completed the handover, I was already standing and waiting to walk to the plane, I was weak and requiring assistance. I asked for the nasal tube to be taken out, they wanted to, but said they couldn't, it had to remain in for a bit longer. I contemplated taking it out myself, I was more than ready, I just couldn't handle it anymore.

As I stepped onto the plane the crew apologised, it was in the process of being refurbished, black plastic covered the walls and much of the seating area. I wasn't bothered by this one bit, to me it was the most beautiful aircraft I'd ever seen!

I was strapped to a bed and the paramedic mentioned that he needed to make his own preliminaries of my condition before take-off. I was offered to go to either Cairns or to the Sunshine Coast, I didn't care—they were both

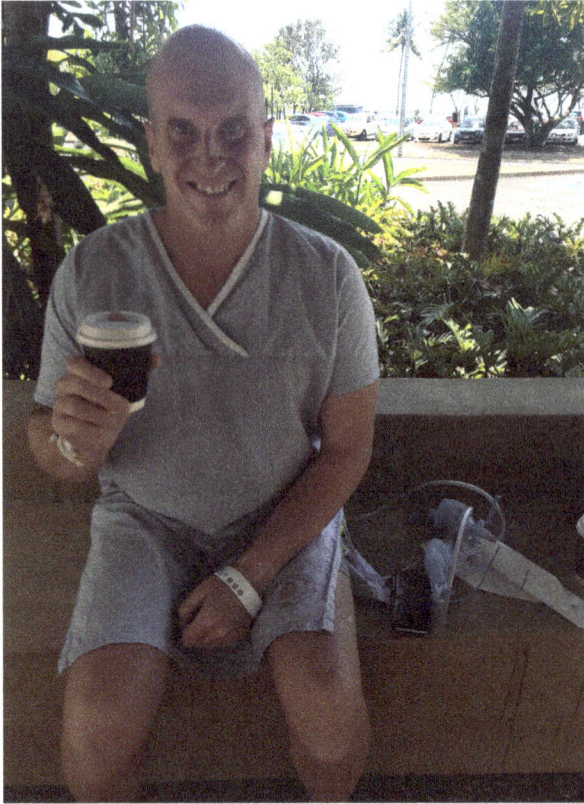

I'd lost 23 kilograms by the time I left hospital three weeks after this ordeal began.

Allowed outside for the first time in weeks, and with my nose tube finally removed, I was allowed to drink something, the best hot chocolate I ever tasted.

Whilst the nose tube was gone, I had surgical drains, you can see them beside me on the bench.

in Australia! He then asked to take my temperature and advised me that if my temperature was high, that I would be going straight to Cairns, the additional time in the air flying to the Sunshine Coast was a risk. He stuck the thermometer into my ear, as soon as it was in, he didn't wait for the final measure, his head snapped towards the pilot and said 'Cairns! And as fast as you can do it!' He then showed the temperature to his colleague with him in the back, while I couldn't see the temperature, her reaction told me it was high.

As we taxied to take off, I was given the instructions about what was required of me. They advised me that they couldn't go to altitude as I had an abdominal issue, and that if I began to feel any pain or discomfort in my abdomen above what I already had, I had to notify them immediately. We were set to go—I was ready to end this nightmare!

Do you remember the last time you were just so happy that you could burst into tears with happiness? Well, that was me the moment the wheels left the tarmac. It was now dark in the city, and I could see the lights out of the window, watching them disappearing into the distance as we got to the altitude that I could fly at. I just remember feeling the tears of happiness falling from my face. The paramedic said, 'you look happy mate, you must have been through an ordeal?' I replied, 'you have no idea!'

I was asked my current pain number out of 10, I replied, 'two to three'. He laughed, 'Yeah right! I've heard about you, your sister told us whatever you said, to quadruple it! I'm writing eight to nine!' Lainie had mentioned to them not to believe me. She believes more than me that I have a high pain tolerance, I thought I was a two—I'd been in more pain than this over the past few days!

They replaced the cannula with their own. The joy I felt in having one less thing in my body that reminded me of that hospital, I was happy having an Australian cannula in my arm, I asked once again about the nose tube—still no.

During the flight, I tried sleeping, but they needed me awake, and to keep me awake they got me talking. Anyone who knows me, knows that it doesn't take much to get me to talk, but in times like this it can be a tougher challenge. They began asking me the series of events, they seemed genuinely amazed by it all. To me it seemed like an unbelievably wild and far-fetched story, they agreed. Within a few moments I would see the lights of Cairns; I was starting to feel pain in my stomach, but they seemed not too bothered knowing how close we were to landing.

There was an ambulance waiting for me, I was off loaded and had to look up for the customs official to check my face against the picture on my passport. She joked about the lack of nose tube in the passport picture—if only she knew how close I was to ripping it out. The paramedic informed me that his office would notify the family where I was; Mum and Mike, Lainie's husband, would come to me. By the time I landed, plans were in place for their travel—they would arrive tomorrow night. For now, I didn't care, I was with Australians, life was as good as it could be.

At the hospital I was led immediately into a room and placed onto a bed. I met with an ER doctor and asked to provide the entire story from the start—he requested an x-ray on my lungs and other scans as seen fit. Collected and wheeled to x-ray, I was asked to stand and to lean against a board, I had to take as deep a breath as I could. I couldn't! What the hell has happened to me, why can't I take a deep breath and hold it? They were unable to x-ray me.

Placed back onto my bed and wheeled down the hall to a room that contained a large cylindrical machine. I was asked to stand up and then lay on the bed within the cylinder. I was asked to my allergies, to which I said, 'nasal tubes' much to the laugher of the Radiographer who said she wasn't taking it out. Instructed on the machine and briefed I may feel like I've wet my pants, that I shouldn't worry, it was the contrast dye they were filling me with via my new cannula. The scan was uneventful and yes, it did kind of feel like I had wet my pants—while I knew I hadn't, I still checked to be sure.

I was wheeled back to my room and tried to sleep once again; I asked for a drink—and yet again I can only have ice. I managed to doze for a bit when a doctor walked in and woke me, she advised me that I'd ruptured my appendix and my abdomen was gangrenous. She informed me that she had to wake the senior surgeon—I needed emergency surgery. A nurse arrived to insert a catheter, a thought that would have once worried me, but for now I thought 'is that all! Bring it, I can handle that, I have a nose tube!'

At 2am I was taken to the surgical ward and told to wait, I was ready, lets do this! Before I knew it, it was 4am and I was woken once again and informed there was a major complication with my condition, it required greater assessment with even more senior surgical staff. Without knowing the complications, I was happy that someone knew what was wrong with me and it was being dealt with. With now no real threat to my life, I drifted straight back to sleep.

At the 6am shift change I was informed it wouldn't be long until I was taken to surgery—there remained no concern from me. At 10am I was advised the surgeon would be in shortly with his team to go over the preliminaries. I was to be weighed for the anaesthetist, being told that this surgery is 'pretty fast' and that I will only be 'out' for a little while.

Asked what I normally weigh, '100 kilograms', I am placed on the scales. A week ago, prior to flying on the charter to Kokoda I was 100 kilograms. I stood on the scales to see the number climbing way past 100, stopping on 115 kilograms! I was a balloon! It turned out the only thing that kept me alive was the significant quantities of antibiotics the hospital in Port Moresby had pumped into me. What the hell—115 kilograms!

Hours passed before I was asked to shower, the surgeon finally came to see me. He informed me there was significant damage to my insides from the rupture and the eight days of infection. I was informed that this was not going to be straightforward, but he was happy to proceed. At 4pm I was taken to surgery for what was now to be an operation of an unknown period of time.

I called the family and let them know what was happening, they let me know that Mike and Mum had left for the airport, they'd be flying from Sydney to Cairns at any moment.

So long and complicated was the operation, that as soon as I woke in recovery Mum and Mike were in the room with me. Drugged, I checked, and the nose tube was still in, but I had a popsicle—it was the first thing I'd eaten in nine days; it was the best popsicle I'd ever tasted! I was taken back to my room to rest, it was after midnight, I was in surgery for six and a half hours.

The surgeon came to see me. He advised me they had a terrible time trying to fix my appendix. The gangrene filling my abdomen had rotted the site of my appendix, and every time they tried to stitch the area, it fell apart. Further, he said it took six litres of fluid to flush the infection from my body and that not only did I now have five key holes in my abdomen, but I also now had two abdominal drains.

I was in more of a mess than I believed. The surgeon said I was 'a very lucky boy', and how if I wasn't as fit as I was, and if I hadn't arrived at the hospital when I did, I'd be dead. That's now twice I've heard that statement in a matter of months, my chances were running out. Mum and Mike were there when the surgeon came, the cost of the plane may have been $40,000 AUD, but it saved my life.

I was in hospital for 12 days, losing 23 kilograms from my pre-surgery weight. Mum stayed and sat with me every day, going back to her hotel to rest at night, only to come back and sit with me for the duration of the following day. I worked hard at recovering, using a lung training device I'd been given—they wanted to increase my lung capacity because of the pneumonia. It had a ball in a tube, I had to suck on a hose to make the ball rise in the tube. I was frustrated, the gauge went to 5000, but I could only get it to 1500. A few days of doing this up to ten times a day, which fatigued me as much as running a marathon, I managed to get it to 3500.

The nurses kept telling me that I had to do it more often, one nurse saying that she hadn't seen me doing it at all. When I said I was frustrated with it because I could only get it to 3500. She yelled at me, 'What! I put the scale to 2000, what do you mean 3500?' I laughed and suggested she not give me something that went to 5000 if she didn't want me to work towards achieving that. She shook her head.

Apart from working on my lung tube, I would take my drain bags in my arms and walk around the ward. One lap would have been 150 metres, so I was aiming for 7 laps to do a kilometre. The first time I tried I could only walk a quarter of a lap. I looked out of the window as I rested before walking back to my room, I could see the Cairns Ironman course. I reflected on six years prior, I ran a marathon there, having ridden 180 kilometres—here I was struggling to walk 50 metres. Though frustrated, I was inspired. I went back to my room to rest; I would try again that afternoon. By the time I left the hospital, I was up to five laps, I was content that once again I was on the path to recovery.

I was hot, I asked Mum to open the window to let the breeze in—I wanted to feel the wind. She looked at me like I was an idiot, saying to me 'hospital windows don't open'. Of course, they don't! Sterility! I reflected on my hospital room in Port Moresby where they did, the dusty winds would come through the window. I know one thing; I was happy to be here with my mum in Australia with first-world medical treatment.

The months passed and my recovery was slow. The trekking season finished with other people leading my treks, but I still had to go back to facilitate the shopping and logistics. It was a strange sensation flying back for the first time. I was anxious, but I knew I wouldn't go back to that hospital again, it just wasn't happening.

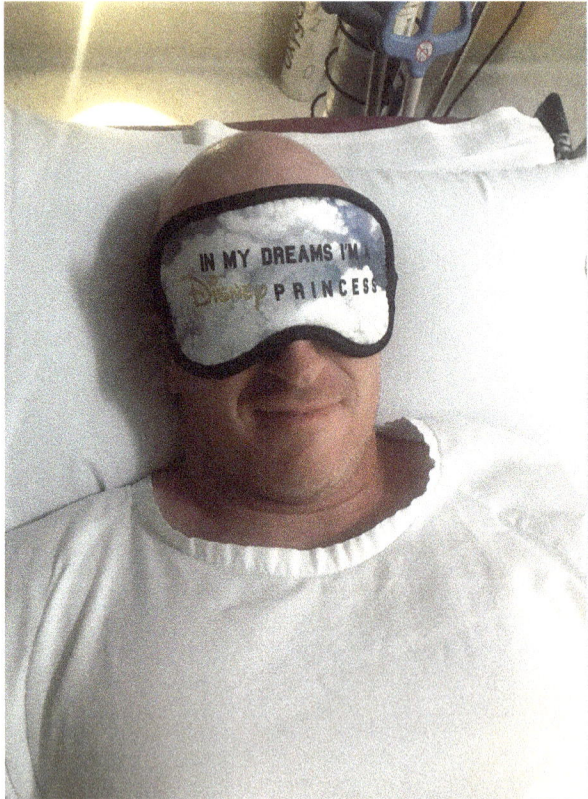

My niece Tania gave this to me to help me sleep, I had to wear it at least once.

WHY I LOVE KOKODA

If you want to know what it feels like to be Australian, visit Brigade Hill.
Bill James'
Kokoda Track Field Manual

Kokoda is one place that most Australians have heard of in some capacity. While the pre-conceived image of some is correct, the reality for many others is a pleasant surprise.

People understand Kokoda to be a jungle track where Australia fought the Japanese in World War 2. They know it to be steep and muddy mountains, which for a portion of the year it is. That said, it can also be very dry too. It's not always the image we see in war time photos—that of people sliding up and down massive mountains in ankle deep mud.

One of the main reasons I love Kokoda—more than the story of supreme sacrifice in the protection of both Australia and Papua—it's also the story of a brotherhood. The relationship between the Australians and the local indigenous population remains as strong today as it was in 1942.

At the start of every trek, I stand with my assigned 'Trek Master' (the most senior guy from our team of local labour) to detail to the clients just how strong and relevant this relationship is.

I explain how in 1942, the Australian soldiers needed the local men (whom they called 'Fuzzy Wuzzy Angels' due to their fuzzy or curly hair), to carry stores and equipment forwards to the battlegrounds. We also needed them to carry the wounded backwards for medical treatment from the doctors and nurses. The locals needed us to help protect their families, and we needed their assistance with carrying. Without each other, neither would have been safe from the Japanese who were intent on destruction.

Today, we need this same assistance to facilitate treks across Kokoda. We need the locals to help us carry our stores forward, and they need us to come and experience their lands, that is, so they can take their wages back home to their families. This relationship goes a long way to the psychology of the man. A man who with this employment feels as though he's contributing to a better life for his family.

Many people don't know this, but Papua New Guinea has a 90% unemployment rate, and there is no welfare. What this means for the men of the trail, who are all direct descendants of the Fuzzy Wuzzy Angels, is they're reliant upon the trekking industry for financial benefit. Further to the labour they offer, the families run market stalls in the villages, selling souvenirs in addition to drinks, snacks, fresh fruits, and vegetables to the passing trekkers. As a company, we purchase so many of the items we require directly from the villages, it helps to boost their economy. Plus, we benefit in that we get the freshest, and most delicious fruits and vegetables you've ever eaten.

A porter will earn the equivalent of two months wages of the average employee in Port Moresby, that's in one trek! What this means is that being a porter is a highly sought-after position, especially when you consider there is no specialised training course—there's no formal qualification.

This is a role that's taken with the utmost seriousness, especially for the 'Personal Porters'. A Personal Porter is one who walks with a client, carrying their heavy pack, allowing the client to walk with a smaller day pack. The Personal Porters assist the clients with where to walk, and where required, support them from physically falling.

Over the years I have watched a Personal Porter belittled in one of the four languages my team speaks for a 'failing', that is, when a client has fallen. If a client has been injured from a fall, the internal counselling the team conducts is almost brutal, where great shame has been thrust amongst the team as a collective. I've had Personal Porters seek to resign over their adventurer being injured; it breaks my heart, as mostly, the client fell in a location that nobody could have foreseen or predicted, usually it's happened quickly too. While I know there was nothing that the porter could have done to have prevented the fall, the team has voted that the porter should have known better, and they have to go—they take it this seriously.

When they're connecting with their 'Adventurer' as we call clients, the boys will start to sing as they walk, some even playing guitars, it lifts the mood of the group and around camp.

Noting the pride they take in their role, it's funny to watch the men in a group together. 'The boys' as they call themselves love to sing, and a great sign for me is the more they sing. I liken them to kids, not in a rude way, but a happy child will talk and sing, and a sad child will be quiet; the 'boys' are much the same. When they're connecting with their adventurer, the boys will start to sing as they walk, some even playing guitars, it lifts the mood in the group and around camp.

I laugh every time a client brings a ball to play with the kids from the villages. The clients will get the ball to kick or pass it with the kids. Before too long, the porters are playing too, and when they've finished, more often than not the ball disappears—only to re-appear with the porters playing by themselves. They bring me so much joy.

One of the most inspiring things for me is seeing the relationships forged between client and porter. Many people who come to Kokoda want to carry their own pack and to 'do it like the soldiers did', and to a point I think this is a brilliant idea. Where I don't think it's a good idea is that they're missing out on one of the greatest aspects of this trek, the involvement and the relationships that are built with the guy walking with you and helping you; you're helping him too! While you're learning about him and his life, he's learning about you and yours also. Nick's first porter was Joseph, who only speaks three languages. The one that he's missing from the four is English!

For nine days I watched Nick and Joseph talking to one other in two separate languages, getting to the point that they each understood the other. I will always smile as I walk into the village called '1900', as it's 1900m above sea level. I think of Nick calling to Joseph, 'C'mon Joseph, lets run', and Joseph yelling out 'we're running', literally the first words in English I've ever heard him speak. I still laugh thinking about Joseph taking off carrying a heavy pack, chasing a 120kg man down a hill.

Amusingly with Joseph, while the only other word I have heard him talk in English is 'yes', I watch him singing hymns in English. He doesn't know how to use the words that he sings in the songs in a spoken sentence, but he knows the words and when to sing them in a song. Interestingly though, he now understands English, and I understand Tok Pisin, one of the languages he speaks. While I can speak Tok Pisin, my accent is too thick for him to understand, so he will talk to me in Tok Pisin, and I will talk to him in English—we can follow the conversation. This brings great amusement to many people, especially Drew, when he witnessed it for the first time, he just kept laughing at the weirdest conversation he'd ever heard.

The two most common questions I'm asked: when is the best time is to walk Kokoda? and which direction? Honestly, neither matters. No matter when you decide to go and which direction you choose, it's the same trail. I love them equally and for a range of reasons. I never leave a trek wishing I'd gone the other direction, and I've never wished the weather

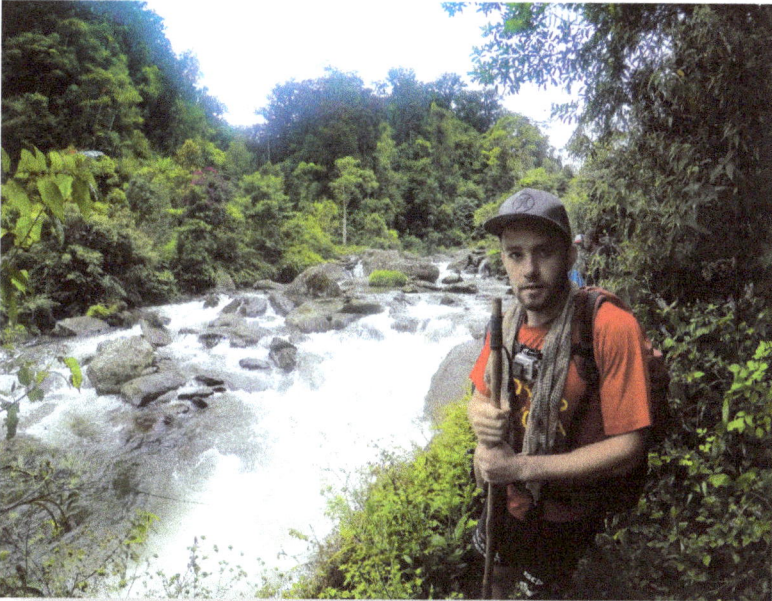

The Trek Master came to me early morning to tell me 'The bridge is not good'. I laughed and said, 'we've been here all night and you're telling me this now?' 'Yes' he replied, we'd have to walk through it.

Adventurer Ben having just walked through the fast-flowing Eora Creek.

had been different, ok, maybe one ANZAC trek when it rained for seven straight days—but!! This is what I love about it, it's always different—no two of my 30 crossings (to this point) have become close to being the same.

The question that I find more interesting is when my favourite time to walk Kokoda is—I have two favourite times.

The first trek of the year is traditionally a wet track. Coming out of the monsoon the jungle is overgrown—it looks raw and looks as though you're one of the first people to ever walk this trail. The villages look less maintained—they haven't had a need to keep them looking fresh—there has been no passing traffic for four months. The porters are super excited to be walking again and the villagers too are excited, this crossing lets them, know that the trekking season is upon them and it's time for them to make some money again.

One of the best things about this trek from my perspective is when the monsoonal rains have washed away the bridges. This means we have to get into the water to cross the fast-flowing rivers—it's like there are fast and heavy pounding waterfalls in the rivers.

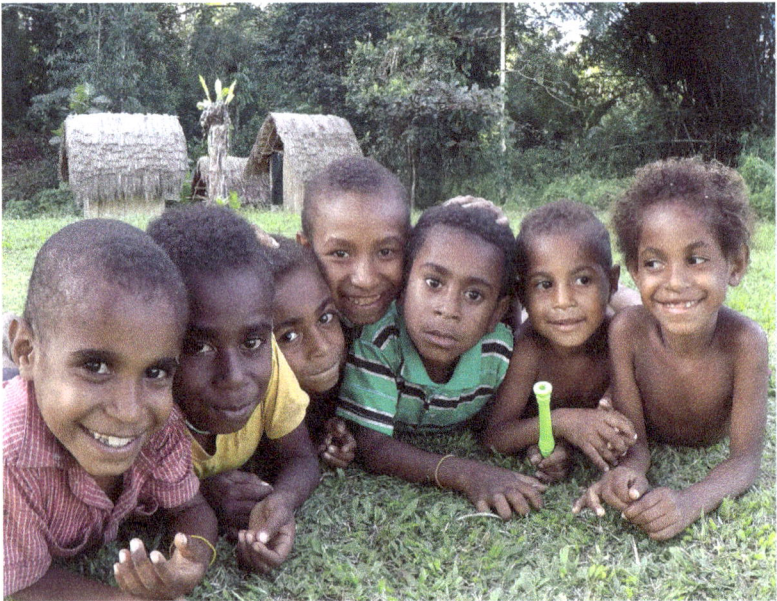

The kids of Kokoda

The thrill and the adventure of being in the jungle with such obstacles excites the hell out of me. Each year I start this trek carrying more ropes and steel clips for the river crossings. I love watching the excitement building within the porters as they approach a river. I love watching them debate in increasing volume to the best way to attack a problem, and I love to watch them decide who is crossing the river first. This is something their families have been doing for generations, and we get to see it first-hand. It's impressive, hilariously funny and the thrill of your life.

I remember in March 2017 standing at the remnants of the bridge in Eora Creek. If you've been to Kokoda and you've seen Eora Creek normally, imagine double the water and quadruple the noise. If you've not been there, imagine Niagara Falls in a creek!

The Trek Master came to me early in the morning to tell me 'The bridge is no good'. I laughed and said to him, 'we've been here all night and you're telling me this now?' 'Yes'—I had to laugh.

I briefed the clients, and we took our shoes off. My lead man, who fronts the treks, Jag, attached himself to a rope and started lowering himself into the frigid waters. Together, he and I looked at where we assessed his best chances of crossing and surviving were.

We moved upstream into a deeper section of water; the deeper the water, the slower it moves, but we couldn't go too deep, we needed him to be able to walk across, he needed to be able to stand—not being able to stand would have been catastrophic.

On the near bank, we moved close to 20 metres upstream from where we wanted him to exit the far bank, he had about 20 metres of river to cross, so you can imagine the angle and the speed of the water. Near the chosen exit point we could see the water started to get fast again, the depth was clearly far shallower, this would allow the clients to stand, but we couldn't muck around in that section; if we did and let slip, people and or their belongings would be pinballing between the river boulders. It was a dangerous predicament, but we mitigated the risk as far as we could.

I held onto the end of the rope, if I had to, I'd pull Jag back to the safety of this bank. I said, 'show us what you got brother!', and with that, his smile widened, and he took off, screaming as the freezing water covered his body. This dude wasn't walking it, he started swimming, what the hell!

Jag also didn't go on the angle, he swam straight across, but I realised quickly what he was doing, he wanted to hit the point we'd chosen as the exit point, which he nailed to perfection.

Having tied his end of the rope to a tree and me the same on the near bank, I decided that I had to make the crossing myself. I needed to lead the way for the clients, to show them it was possible. I also had to walk it, noting Jag swam, which would show the clients that you didn't have to swim it. I also had to check to assess if it was too dangerous, if I believed it was, we'd have to find another way.

I set off, walking deeper into the fast, freezing water. Having negotiated some slippery rocks, I made it, it was safe to pass, but the cool morning

Standing on the northern side of Brigade Hill.
This is the valley that Australian soldiers fought thousands of Japanese in the
Battle of Brigade Hill.

breeze across my wet clothes from the freezing waters dropped my core temperature quickly. We had to get everyone and everything across the river quickly before any of us got hypothermia.

Having successfully crossed the clients, we now had to get their packs across. We watched the commotion as the team threw packs and ropes across the river, watching something eject from a pack as it thudded into the ground. I saw the horror on Obed's face—he'd been carrying and had thrown the pack. Out of the corner of my eye Jag took off like an Olympic sprinter at full speed—he transitioned into James Bond-like jumping from boulder to boulder until he launched himself head-first into the most turbulent section of water, slamming his back into the rocks and so close to plummeting over the falls. He stood up in victory, holding a $5 water bottle. All that stress for a water bottle. I commended his commitment but cautioned him not to do it again.

The other time that I love to trek is the ANZAC period. There are several reasons why I love this trek, but the traffic on the trail and the stress

Three 100% Kokoda groups at Isurava for ANZAC in 2019, a special occasion for them and also for me, but for a different reason. My dream of multiple concurrent treks was now a reality

to me as a company owner and as a guide is definitely not one of them. Let me detail the reasons why I don't love this trek before I tell you all the reasons why it's a favourite.

As a company owner there is no way to book campsites for the trail. It's a 'first in, best dressed' arrangement. Traditionally, group sizes are larger than usual and there are more groups to contend with. So, bigger sized and a greater quantity of groups—meaning campsites are severely limited.

As there is no way to book, I don't know who is going to be out there—I can't plan. It's not until I'm standing in the welcome hall in the international airport on the day prior to a trek commencing that I get any idea who will be out there with me.

Typically, there is a lot of 'which way are you going' followed by 'where are you staying' and a lot of informal chatter between the companies—all trying to work out who will go where and when. There will be the companies that want to work with us, and there will be the ones that don't, but overall, when you give a little, you get back somewhere too.

I've found the last few times I've facilitated this trek that we've had a few busy days early on, that's until the crowd settles, and everyone finds their own space. Then we come across the groups headed in the other direction, then we're all once again fighting for space and having the same issues. It can be quite stressful as a company owner and as a guide—it can take close to a week before I can relax. This is why I don't like it!

For the clients, as most companies follow a similar schedule you start to get recognition with the people in the other groups. You will meet someone from another trek waiting for a shower or a toilet, or swimming in a river. You will see these people over the course of your trek, and you start to build a rapport with them too.

In 2019 we came across Greg. When I first saw him on day two of his trek, he looked the worse for wear. But, each day, our group said hello to him, getting to know his name and getting to be a part of his journey too. The reason he was having a tough time was that he was close to having a double knee replacement; he figured that he may as well fully ruin the knees he had before getting them replaced, so it was the time to do Kokoda.

He became a talking point in our group, and everyone fed from his positivity. Everyone stopped complaining about their own ailments as they took inspiration from Greg.

When you get to the battlefield at Isurava, which is where you spend the night prior to ANZAC Day, there is a real carnival atmosphere. There are people everywhere. People who have come from both directions, with some just starting their journey and on day two, while others are on day seven or eight.

For 100% Kokoda, we traditionally have treks in both directions over the ANZAC period. We have both a 9 and a 10-day trek. These leave Port Moresby a day apart and walk towards Kokoda. Then we have a 9-day trek from Kokoda, walking towards Port Moresby—all arriving at the battleground on the same afternoon, 24 April. We have one massive campsite and we come together as a community to commemorate this special occasion.

What I love about it is that it lets people feel a part of something far greater than their own trek. They are a part of a community. It's on this night that we have a massive cook up, we all eat together, porters included, and we all mingle, meeting new people from our team. You will see others from other companies, but the 100% crew just seems to stick together, I love it!

The following morning prior to the commencement of the Dawn Service, we host our own Gunfire Breakfast, where we share war-time stories, and play some apt music over a rum filled coffee with ANZAC biscuits. Traditionally the clients wear their red 100% Kokoda trekking shirts, and they have all by this stage received their 100% Kokoda beanie, these are worn by most as they stand together to partake in the service.

It's such a thrill to stand there as the owner of a brand, to see these people embracing what you have strived to create. It fills my heart to see the team of porters, stand with the clients, every one of them in their black 100% Kokoda porter shirts—the mix of colours represent the colours of Papua New Guinea.

Best of all, it almost made me want to cry with pride when the service concluded, a hymn started behind us—it was our porters with the porters of a friend's company, serenading the crowd. To see people from all companies watching proudly, I shared their pride and was delighted that the porters clearly understood what I am trying to achieve. I love that they're buying into this culture too. It's for these reasons that I love this trek.

That final day on the trail is one of celebration. We find that by the time we get to the village of Deniki, which is the first time that those walking to the north will see Kokoda, the mood seems to somehow lift even more. Once we've descended the final hill to the village of Hoi, it's time to sit in the warmer waters with some fresh pineapple and play ball games with the kids.

That afternoon you're only completing two kilometres of flat walking to camp, so there's time to really relax and embrace the mood of the group.

Rachael, Jennie and Beck celebrating the completion of their trek at the Kokoda Airfield in the village of Kokoda.

To explain how special this trek is, we have the same people returning each year to walk the same trail in the same direction, albeit with a slightly different team—but they just love it. To them, it's the time that they can embrace nature, often bringing others with them to share this experience.

The final morning when we fly from Kokoda back to Port Moresby, you will see groups of people standing at the airfield with a beer, laughing with their own group and with other people they've met along the way. For me, this is when I can really relax and embrace the history, culture and the happiness of the people around me. I just love it.

100% WORLD WIDE ADVENTURES

A diamond is a chunk of coal that did really well under pressure.
Henry Kissinger

The plan for the business was always to expand from more than just Kokoda. I started with Kokoda because that's what I knew. In our infancy I was content with this being the only available travel option, but the more time I spent in New Guinea, the more I realised how foolish it would be to put all of my 'eggs into one PNG basket.' The reason for this is because in Papua New Guinea, a single incident—even one outside of my control (and there are many of those)—could put the entire survival of the business at risk.

What this meant was that that one single incident, not necessarily related to 100% Kokoda, but on Kokoda or within the country itself, stood to compromise the trekking industry and therefore any ability to maintain the company—not to mention, earn an income and support myself.

The Army gave me financial security, but here I was in the travel industry and in this country, with little to no security and a real threat to business longevity. It didn't take me too long to start thinking of the range of other adventures I wanted to do. I wanted our future destinations to be ones that not only I wanted to see and conquer, but that other people would too. I started dreaming bigger.

Many years prior I'd seen a program on hiking to Everest Base Camp. The trekkers had alternating nights between tents and tea houses, stopping at the Everest View Hotel for a beer—this was my type of hike. It had adventure, and it had a level of comfort. Inspired, I knew I would one day complete this hike.

I decided this was to be the next brand under the 100% banner—I registered the name 100% Everest. Then, as I had met so many people who had completed and raved about Kilimanjaro, I registered that name too. I also wanted something to cover everything else that didn't fit under one of the other titles—I decided on 100% Adventure to achieve this. This was also registered and added to the list.

I wanted to see Everest and I was really excited at the thought of not only doing this trek myself, but facilitating treks in this destination under our new banner—it's a hugely popular destination. I knew that, unlike Kokoda, where you complete this trek with either an Australian or a PNG based company, in Nepal I would be competing with companies from around the world. Not necessarily a big issue, as I knew many of the people who'd trekked Kokoda with me liked our model, they knew what to expect from a 100% branded adventure.

While I knew I was now competing within an international market and against many US based companies, I also knew I was building a profile within Australia, and how those Australian based people would like the fact that they were paying for this adventure in Australian dollars.

What this means is that they're not paying for the cost of their trek against the sliding US dollar, which is what they would be doing if they chose to trek with an offshore company. This includes Nepalese based companies who scale their trek fees in US dollars. I knew our Australian clients would like to know that by choosing us to facilitate their Nepalese adventure, they were protected by Australian consumer laws. This was an attractive element for this market.

The plan for me to travel to Nepal and facilitate this adventure was set. I had liaised with local contacts, seeking the best people to assist me with local labour, logistics and indigenous guides. Some of the people I liaised with seemed ok, but then I met a lady who, along with her husband, ran logistics that could support my operation. I discovered their thinking aligned with mine. Like me, they were a smaller 'boutique' operation, so I would fly to meet them, together with my nephew Lachlan. We would meet and then complete the trek that I so desperately wanted to sell. This was a great opportunity to see it for myself, capture the imagery and take it to market. But, I contracted malaria and then ruptured my appendix, I was devastated—I had to postpone.

Months passed and my desire to do this trek didn't diminish, it only got stronger. I needed to get to Nepal. With my health coming back, I was going; not to walk it this time, that would come later, but this time I would go to meet with the logistics team, finalise our costings, and show them I was serious to make this dream a reality.

In my first season as 100% Kokoda, a guy called Nick Fife trekked with me as a client. Nick and I had become great friends, remaining in contact, and catching up where able to discuss life, business and a mutual sharing of ideas. We loved to work on opportunities to improve, streamline and capitalise in our respective businesses.

Nick ran a financial management and legal conveyancing business; he spent a lot of time on the road in both regional New South Wales and in Canberra. He would randomly drop into the house, have a coffee and over the course of a few months, the ideas he was offering were making headway within my current business model. I said to him on one occasion how I was financially unable to remunerate him for his professional guidance— he didn't want payment, helping me was a nice distraction from his own business, a business that he was in the early stages of selling.

It was on one such day that I flippantly said, 'if you do all of this for free, what would you do if you were in the company', a comment that caught him by surprise—to be honest, even though it came out of my mouth, it caught me by surprise too. Was I serious? No, I wasn't, but then again, maybe I was?

I asked him to socialise the idea with his wife, we'd come back to it. If he did come into the business though, in what capacity would this be? I didn't know.

A week passed and the idea of taking Nick on as a partner kept coming back to me. How would it work? Would I want it to work? I know I work for myself as a sole trader; but, with my current model and facilitating everything myself, I'd never be able to expand to the level I wanted, a level I believed possible.

100% Everest, now a subordinate company to the headquarters of 100% World Wide Adventures taking its maiden voyage into Nepal.

Being greeted by our Hotel Host 'Hari' upon our arrival in Kathmandu. We were all bursting with excitement.

With self-assessment, I could keep taking a maximum of 110 people across Kokoda each year, but by doing this alone, I had no capacity to offer another trek, no ability to invest into the other destinations. At the current rate, I'd be lucky to be able to do one Everest Base Camp a year, my schedule on Kokoda and the additional load of administration was just so tight. If I remained at this point, there would be no advancement—100% Everest and 100% Kilimanjaro would only ever be my 'travel hobbies'.

I knew if I didn't have Nick on the team, I would have to employ someone to be able to grow. I would need to be able to trust them, but I also knew an employee wouldn't be as invested in the business as I was—a partner however would be. I knew the people who came to Kokoda, generally departed seeking their next adventure. I needed to inspire them while I had their attention.

If I didn't have a partner or an employee that I could trust, then frankly, no other destination would get off the ground. The market was there for it, I knew I needed help to expand.

My mind was racing, not even I could keep up with it—I needed to clear my head—I went for a run. I returned in the same mindset, now just sweaty and no further advanced than I was before. I was overwhelmed with thoughts of future projections, target markets and endless possibilities, but what was the right option for me and my 'baby'—100%.

I was starting to see the possibilities of taking Nick on as a partner. He loved the space, he had the financial knowledge to take the brand into the next phases of growth and beyond, he had the legal background, he had a business acumen far greater than mine. His ability to calculate numbers off the top of his head is incomprehensible. He would enable the business to grow.

I ran my own numbers in my head. I could make this much each year from taking 100 people across Kokoda, with no ability to grow and working hard all year by myself. But by taking Nick on as a partner, while on the surface I would lose half of the earnings, it would allow me to grow organically, and exponentially, possibly making three to four times these earnings in each of the coming years. This would at least double my potential earnings.

Further, it will allow me to grow the brand to an unknown point and will also be a reduction in my time investment, freeing my time to do other things. I thought again, I could double my earnings and reduce my time investment, that's compared to where I am presently, without him.

I'm currently at capacity. I go over it in my head once again then think, 'I'm about to launch 100% World Wide Adventures' as the over-arching headquarters to the four 100% brands within it. I picked up the phone to call Nick; the decision was made as far as I was concerned.

I called Nick and formally asked him to join me in the business—he was stoked, he was in! He'd discussed it with his wife and had her full backing, she was happy for him to take on this challenge. To her, it would mean he would be away from home a lot more, but when he was at home, he would be in the house, not in his office until late at night, merely a few kilometres away from where his wife and kids were at home waiting for him. His new office would be the world.

One of Nick's first tasks as a business partner was to accompany me on this trip to Nepal. We'd fly together and make the necessary arrangements, prior to heading back to Nepal in December to complete the trek.

We had a brilliant time, it was a trip that we not only learnt a lot more about each other, but we learnt a lot about dealing with the Nepalese.

The Nepalese are a proud nation of people who are big into business, but overall, they're not too keen on having the hard discussions where financial decisions need to be made. Together we realised that without trying to be, we were culturally confronting in our approach to these discussions.

Having explained the reasoning for certain things—namely Australian governance requirements—our Nepalese hosts realised we weren't taking advantage of them. They soon realised, we were protecting ourselves as an Australian owned company, compliant with Australian consumer and taxation laws, albeit working in a foreign nation.

Having made our way home from Nepal, we knew we'd be back in a matter of months to hike to Base Camp, with great mate, Larry.

The months passed and the excitement grew, preparing to finalise the Kokoda trekking season would mean it was almost time for us to hit the Himalaya. Filled with excitement for this new adventure. But first, we would have to complete one more Kokoda.

On our final Kokoda for the year, Nick came to walk the trail in the opposite direction to what he had done previously. Having walked Kokoda twice now, both times from north to south, on this trek, he would see the multiple differences in walking the other way.

Larry was also on this trek, having walked Kokoda in April that year; he was there to learn how to guide—this was something he wanted to do into the future. I was excited about this too; I could see Larry being a great fit to join the team of guides. It was a brilliant trek that was marred only by a single incident. One incident, that when it happened, did so in less than half-a-second, and almost took me out of Nepal.

In an attempt to quickly cross a high bridge to capture imagery of the Adventurers standing above the fast-flowing river below, I slipped on the wet and unstable logs. Crossing bridges is a task that I've done literally hundreds of times; but, on this day, I slipped as I looked for the perfect location in relation to the sun. Crossing the bridge, I grabbed the rope acting as a handrail, upon losing my balance, the rope didn't hold as it should, there was too much slack on it, moving with my balance to a point of tension, which was way off the edge of the bridge.

Noting that I was now falling off the side of the bridge, in my mind it felt like the first part of this fall was in slow motion. I vividly recall thinking I would swing my body to grab the rope with my other hand so that I could swing under the bridge, pull myself back up onto it, or drop safely onto the rocks or into the water beneath. The problem was, that as I got to the horizontal position, the rope snapped. Before I knew it, I'd fallen three metres, landing flat on my back onto the rocks below. I hit the ground with such force that the air expelled from my body.

Gilbert, one of our senior porters watched the event unfold. He screamed as I hit the ground, launched from his seat, and ran over to me. I jumped up, ripped open my pack to see that my water bladder had broken, I cared not for that, but I did for the $1500 camera that my 100kg body had just landed on from a good height. Pulling it from the pack, I could see it was still intact, I was happy. I noted that my arms and legs weren't broken, I hadn't even considered that to this point, I was too concerned about the camera. Gilbert was looking intently at a large gash in my shin.

I knew that gash wouldn't stop me doing Everest. I was happy again, and made sure that from that point on, I took absolutely no risks that would prevent my Nepalese dream from becoming a reality.

When I think back to that documentary, I'd watched all those years prior, I was about to experience the very thing that'd inspired me, walking to Base Camp and stopping at Everest View Hotel.

Sitting with good mate Larry, at Everest View Hotel, looking at Mount Everest, toasting the occasion with an 'Everest' branded beer. I was about as happy as a man can be.

LOOKING AT THE TOP OF THE WORLD

Without a goal you can't score.

Unknown

The day to fly back to Nepal had arrived, the three of us were filled with excitement. We met at Sydney airport to fly to Kathmandu through China. We landed in Kathmandu and completed our visas, making our way through customs and waiting for what felt like over an hour for our bags to arrive. When the first of our bags came out, you could feel the relief within the group. We had all quietly started to think our bags were still somewhere in China—bags that contained all of the equipment we required for this adventure.

We made our way out of the airport to see our host, Hari, standing in the crowd on the opposite side of the road. Hari was typically on his phone, waving with a smile so wide that you could see that he was as excited to see us, as we were to see him. Nick and I had met Hari on our last visit to Nepal. He is an amazing man, owning the hotel where we stay, he would be driving us back to what will be our home for the next few days.

We passed through the crowds of people to get to him, shaking hands and back slapping, to have him place orange coloured flower leis around our necks; these would offer us luck on our adventure. The excitement within our small group had built to a new, and somehow even higher level, we were bursting, we were here, we knew that this was at long last about to happen!

We made our way to the hotel, deciding that Larry and I would share a room, leaving Nick with his snoring/sleep talking to himself. We spent the first three days meeting with the team, exploring, sightseeing, and buying the last-minute stores that we both wanted and needed. Sometimes you need to buy the things that you want as much as the things that you need. We were based in the Kathmandu suburb of 'Thamel' (sounds like camel, but with a 'T'). Thamel is the central hub in the city for tourists, and for the people who are in Nepal to hike, climb and do the suite of adventurous activities on offer.

Thamel is an amazing place. If you're interested in these sorts of activities, this is your Mecca. It's a series of streets lined with cafés, bars, restaurants, hiking shops that each sell everything you would ever want or need—all bartering to compete against one another for your business. There are street vendors selling literally everything, there are souvenir shops selling brass goods, a main seller is the 'singing bowls', not to mention shops selling T-Shirts and hats literally everywhere! It's a cultural hotspot and a place that you never tire, you cannot get enough of it, but it does wear a little thin having people following you to sell you something that you 'must have'— even drugs. It's funny, I was always offered drugs, and Nick was offered a lot of massages—I laugh to myself now even writing that.

One of the main things we were unable to do in Australia before we departed was have the 100% Everest badges manufactured to brand our clothing; we couldn't find anyone to do it within the limited time we had available. Walking the streets of Thamel, we noticed a lot of people sewing on the streets. We asked one of them if he could re-produce the 100% Kokoda badge, but to make it say Everest. He gave us a look of 'ah, yeah!' so we gave him the money, a badge and wrote what we wanted it to say, E.V.E.R.E.S.T.

The following day we went to see how he was going; he had sewn them all free hand on a standard sewing machine, they were exactly what

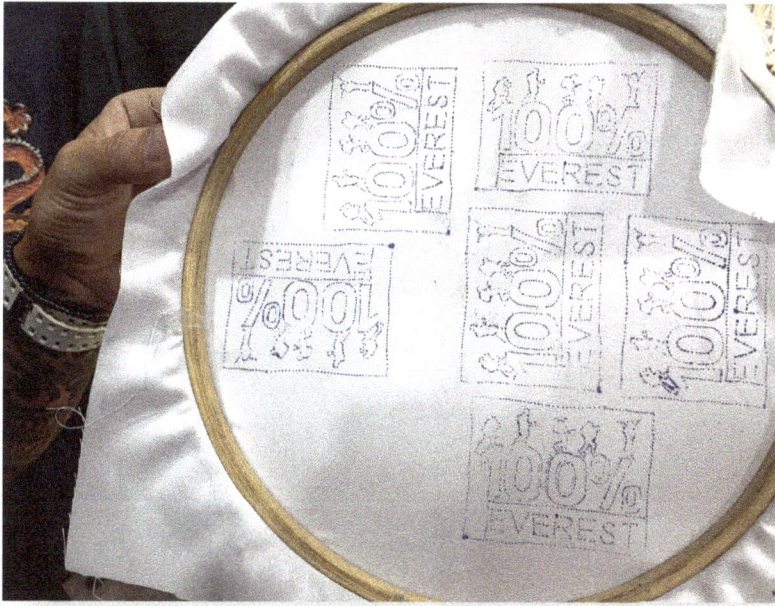

The badge templates which were free hand sewn on the street

we'd asked for. This was no bulk manufacture, he'd hand drawn each of the twenty badges we'd requested, then sewed each individually. Seeing that he was almost done, we quickly ran back to the hotel to grab the clothes we wanted these badges on. This was massive for us, to have branded clothing in the imagery we planned to produce was exactly what we needed to complete this journey. We needed it for the primary purpose of promotion for future clients.

The day arrived for us to commence our adventure. We woke early, bursting with excitement, unsure of exactly what to wear to accommodate the conditions, having been told, 'it can be quite warm at the lower altitudes'. With this information, Nick wore shorts, I wore shorts with 'skins' underneath for some added leg warmth, you know, just in case. Larry was wearing new thermal lined pants he'd been able to acquire in Kathmandu. Nick and I also wanted pants like these, but noting Larry was an extra-large in local sizing, Nick and I had no chance of getting any to fit. Let's say as politely as I can, were a lot 'thicker' in the waist than Larry.

We were met by the bus and our guide, Shiva, who would be our indigenous guide on the trek—our first task was to make the journey from the hotel to the airport. We arrived in the pre-dawn darkness to the sight of a long line of people all dressed as we were. They were all clearly flying to various parts of the country to hike and explore.

Wearing close to everything we owned as we landed in Lukla.
Comically, moments earlier we were in shorts, it was that cold!

We were thankful Shiva was there, he knew exactly where to go and what to do. Having placed our bags through security just to get into the airport, we made our way to the check-in counter of our airline. Shiva waiting with us, and upon our turn to talk, he took charge and did all the talking, taking our bags and asking for cash to pay the excess baggage costs. We were all done—that was too simple, thanks to Shiva. Tickets in hand, we walked to the next security point to proceed through to the gates within the 'terminal'.

Amusingly, Nick had inadvertently left his pocketknife in the bag he would carry onto the plane. With a bit of commotion, Nick was pulled to the side of the line, questioned by security with the offending item removed.

We all wanted a coffee, but Shiva looked jittery, we wondered why, then without a word he walked back to the security point, re-appearing moments later with the knife. I don't know what he said, but so much for the security commotion.

Having boarded our plane, you could feel the excitement, we just wanted to take off and hit the skies—we were ready for our destination, the world's most dangerous airport, Lukla, in the Khumbo Valley. While all excited beyond comprehension, we didn't know what to expect when landing at Lukla. Anyone that has researched this airport, knows the stories of crashed planes that have missed the landing on the side of the hill, the wreckages remain. Just months earlier there had been a crash, so we were acutely aware of this, excited, apprehensive, and ready!

As the plane took off, we were wide eyed and looking at everything. The constant excitement of 'look at that' moments, pointing for the others to see. Flying amidst the snow-covered mountains and wondering when we would see Everest for the first time. Shiva was pointing to things, but with the noise, we couldn't hear him and were none the wiser about what he was pointing at—it was just another mountain in a sea of mountains. We were excited, but without any certainty that what we were looking at was actually Everest. There were just so many mountains in the direction he was pointing—it was likely to be one of the smaller ones, being dwarfed by the closer mountains.

As we started to approach Lukla, you could feel the anticipation build in the cabin, not just ours, but everyone. Cameras were on and videos being taken all around us, everyone wanting to get the footage of the plane landing on this famous runway.

As soon as you think you are about to land, you're not, you start to see the hills right beside the windows when bang! With a thump you land and you're on the ground; all you can see are the mountains all around you— even in front of you as you drive uphill to the taxi area.

As the plane crested the hill and the airport came into view, we saw people loitering on the taxiway, dressed as hikers, and clearly waiting to board the plane we were about to step off.

If you saw the cult movie 'Cool Runnings' about the Jamaican Bobsled team, then this will make some sense to you. Picture the scene when the team arrived in Calgary. Think of the character 'Sanka', walking through the front door of the airport to have the snow and mist hitting him in the face. This was the scene we stepped off the plane to. The wind and the cold air coming off the propellers, made that same mist.

Nick and I walked behind the plane, to be greeted by at least fifty people staring opened mouthed and pointing at us. Remembering that Nick was wearing shorts. There were looks ranging from horror to great amusement.

We collected our bags and made our way to a tea house on the opposite side of the airport. We were met by two locals who took Nick and Larry's bags and headed off at great speed. I was left to carry my own bag, joking that the Director of the company was the only one actually doing it.

I was just open eyed and open mouthed, I was here! I was about to start the trek that I had dreamed of doing above all others; I cannot begin to explain the excitement running through my body at that point. As we walked to the tea house, we passed the top end of the runway, a plane was postured and preparing to take off. This is one of those places where an image does no justice. I had seen a lot of images and a lot of videos too (which I wouldn't recommend prior to landing here). The runway looks steep in a photo, but from above it where I was standing, it's straight downhill prior to going off a cliff ledge.

I took in this moment to myself. I could feel the freezing air streaming off the propellers of the plane. The engine roared and then almost screamed prior to the brakes being released—the plane taking off straight downhill and out of sight—it just disappeared, re-appearing a matter of seconds later and making its way through the valley below. I stood in awe and shook my head—I was just so happy to be here.

To my right I saw Nick, who was now wearing what appeared to be the contents of his bag, it looked as though he was wearing everything that he owned. I couldn't help but laugh how the boy from one of the coldest towns in Australia, was finally cold. What we knew, was that we both needed new gloves, what we'd brought was either too much or not enough for what we were about to undertake.

The trip was everything and more that I hoped it would be. The culture, the people, and the insane ways that they live. We all loved the trekking, but it was the people and the scenery that made it amazing. We would stop whenever we felt like it—just sitting in awe of the mountains that surrounded us. We found ourselves following or passing trains of mules or yaks as they carried stores and equipment up and down the paths. We watched time and again as they passed over the steel bridges that sit incomprehensibly high above the freezing waters below.

Larry's failed Sherpa audition. Note the size of the boy to the right, it was his load that Larry tried to lift, much to the young man's amusement.

On the second day of walking, we walked to a village called Namche Bazaar, which is approximately 600m in elevation higher than the highest point of Australia. On the way we stopped for a coffee, we met some men from Brisbane who were walking back to Lukla. They gave us guidance on the things that they'd learnt on their trek, things they wished they'd had known on their way up, like how to preserve battery power in phones and cameras from the extreme cold. It was great information to have, noting that I was not only there to experience it, but to capture the imagery to promote this adventure.

Having departed this tea house, we came across a father and son resting from carrying their heavy loads to Namche. These men are amazing, they carry the heaviest loads through a strap that's placed against their foreheads, all of the weight coming through their necks and upper backs. Why do they carry it this way? I'm guessing it's the way that they have always done it. When you see how much they're carrying, I would assume that they can carry a lot more in their open baskets than they could in a backpack. Regardless, these two were resting and Larry flippantly mentioned that he wanted to carry one. I called out to Shiva and asked him if he could ask if Larry could have a go—this was amusingly agreed to.

Larry is a fit man, physically robust, with a cardio engine that most athletes would be proud to have. He was in no question, the fittest of the three of us. Larry walked over and Shiva offered him to try the young boys load, noting that the young boy would have been no older than 12 years of age. I don't know if it was ego or pride or a combination of both, but Larry said he wanted to carry the father's, which was a large basket filled with boxes of I don't know what.

Leaning against the wall that this basket was resting on, Larry began trying to lift, the strain immediately apparent through his neck as the veins bulged and his face turned instantly red. Nick and I being good mates with Larry, of course were both laughing in hysterics and filmed the ordeal, while not having the courage to have a turn ourselves. Watching Larry's body start to shake uncontrollably once again as he tried in vain for a second time to take the weight of the load—he was unable to shift it at all.

Not to be defeated, he was once again offered the boy's basket, the young man smiled at him almost arrogantly. Larry took the strap, placing it against his forehead. This small human with a beaming smile watched this large foreign man standing with his basket attached to his head. This time Larry had more success in getting the basket off the wall, but clearly, it was still not easy—Larry attempted to take a few steps, each lacking confidence, with an uncontrollable hitch to his gait. Larry, while not victorious, was a long way from defeated, placing the basket back down before he hurt himself. Nick and I laughed uncontrollably and were not having a go at that at all! We were somewhat satisfied that it was clearly a lot harder than it already looked, and that we couldn't do it.

Over the course of the next hour, we climbed in altitude. While still very low to what we would climb in the following days, we were as high in altitude as any of us had ever been. We took it slow, remembering to drink with the 'post-lunch hiking blues' of having cooled down and having all the blood that was once in our legs, now in our stomach.

Taking small steps and leaning into the hill, Shiva had taken us over the 'Hillary Bridge' named after the first man to ascend Mount Everest. It was not far past this that there was a random garbage bin overflowing with litter. I thought it a little odd Shiva would stop us at a bin, until he said 'Look, Everest'. Looking up through the opening in the trees to see it—Mount Everest! We'd seen it! The tallest mountain in the world was right in front of us. Almost screaming and running about, back slapping each other in the excitement, we couldn't contain ourselves; I don't ever recall being so excited in my life. I knew that we were still a long way away from it, and the closer we got, the bigger it would be. I just hoped that I got more excited each time that I saw it.

The following day was an acclimatisation day, where we walked higher in altitude prior to coming back down to sleep. This would help us acclimate more efficiently for the higher altitudes to come. I'd been looking forward to this day in particular, potentially even more than actually getting to Base Camp. This was the day I would get to the Everest View Hotel, the site that I had seen on that video so many years prior. We walked to well-known landmarks such as the statue of Tenzing Norgay, the Sherpa who assisted Sir Edmund Hillary on the first successful ascent of Everest. This statue is in so many images that you see when you research this adventure, it was a thrill to stand there and have a photo of it with Mount Everest behind.

Next stop was the Everest View Hotel! I was beyond excited. We saw runners who were competing in the biennial Hillary Marathon, from Everest Base Camp to Namche Bazaar, they weren't going to stop me. While it was impressive to watch these amazing athletes move with such floating speed across the uneven terrain, I've seen enough endurance events in my life that I didn't really need to see another one. I wanted to visit the hotel and I wanted to see the mountain from this location.

Have you ever had a moment where the more effort you gave to reach a destination, the further you seemed from it? This was that day for me. I wasn't waiting for the boys, they were still watching the runners, I was walking.

I walked slowly and remained within my comfort zone, trying not to burn too much energy. Noting I had never been to these altitudes, I had no idea how my body was going to react the higher we got. I was keeping all my reserves just in case I needed them in the days to come. What I did know, was that many experienced hiking colleagues have struggled and failed at altitude. I didn't know if I would too. I wanted to take this first outing easy, I wanted to see how my body coped and reacted with altitude, knowing depending how I went on this trek, that in future I might be able to push a little harder—I kept it easy this time.

As I approached the hotel, my excitement levels went through the roof, walking into it, reminded me of walking into a ski lodge, it was beautiful. I walked outside and onto the back deck that I have seen in so many images;

to see Everest, from the Everest View Hotel—this moment was everything I'd dreamt about. The only thing that could top this would be an Everest branded beer, at Everest View Hotel, looking at Mount Everest, which Larry and I later did, clicking our drinks together to celebrate the occasion.

The next few days were much the same, there were a lot of laughs and a lot of 'look at that' moments. It seemed that every few minutes one of us was pointing something out and at least three of us taking a photo of it. At the very least, we would have a lot of imagery to use. While I was loving the experience, there was a flip side.

I know this may sound strange, but it's honestly how I felt. We have an amazing community who love and support who we are, and what we do. Thanks to social media, they were genuinely excited to be sharing this experience with us. The negative for me was that throughout the experience, I was never off social media, maintaining this engagement with the community, except for one night—where the tea house where we stayed due to an unexpected stop had no Wi-Fi. That was the only night when I was really able to be in the moment and enjoy the surrounds and the company of the people I was with, not just Nick and Larry, but the Sherpas, and the family who we stayed with.

The positive side of having social media contact with the community, really highlighted how genuinely interested people were in sharing our experience. From a business perspective, it allowed us to generate real time excitement, which in turn sells treks, ultimately, that was the whole point of us being here and socialising our adventure.

The bad and necessary evil for the positives was that it never let me really be in the moment. I am a massive believer in my own saying that 'not everything is for everyone'. What I mean when I say this, is that I honestly believe that an image will detail the natural beauty of a place, and it will show you a setting, but it doesn't really have the same impact as when you stand in front of it, seeing it for yourself and feeling the emotions of that moment. It's for this reason that I will at times prohibit cameras on our treks.

I fell immediately in love with Nepal and the Himalayas.
I found my spiritual home in these mountains.

By prohibiting cameras at these times and taking this option away from the clients, means that they are now truly in the moment. They're making real memories, taking in the beauty and the experience, not looking at it through a lens. Looking at a setting only through a lens means that you capture only a small portion of the experience, you miss out on what I believe to be the entire point of making the effort, spending the money, taking the time off work and for many, the sacrifice of family time.

I believe it's my responsibility to make sure my clients take this time and 'own that space'. Let's be honest, the people you share this imagery with will look at it, think it's amazing, but then look for the next picture you can show them. They didn't invest the money, or take the time or endure the hardships, so to me, always be in the moment and capture it for yourself. I want people to feel the emotion of the setting, not think that they better take a picture to post on a platform for a 'like'.

This was something I struggled with, but again I came to the conclusion that this trek wasn't about me; it was about the clients and the necessity to build as much excitement as I could. So, each day I logged on and did my best to showcase what we were looking at.

This was how my afternoons went. We would arrive at the tea house, Nick and Larry would order a drink and a snack for us; I would be gaining access to Wi-Fi. I would share the password with them, where they would start to send me their best photos of the day. I would start processing imagery as they made calls to loved ones. I would edit the chosen shots,

The way to Everest Base camp is that way!

drink my tea and post the imagery. The boys would still be on their phones as I started to reply to comments, spending up to an hour maintaining the engagement. At some stage, Shiva would tell me that we had to go, we would walk higher in altitude. We would sit for close to an hour before walking back to the tea house for the night. As mentioned previously, this was so we 'walked high/slept low' in altitude, helping us to acclimate for the following day. We treated this daily process quite seriously.

What this meant however, was when we got back to the tea house, I would be back on my phone, replying to more comments before noting that it was now late at home. I could then change into my night clothes and eat dinner before bed. I didn't really get a lot of sitting time, but again, it's not about me, and if it was, that doesn't sell treks. That said, when you're tired, it can be hard to remember this, and I knew that. Upon reflection in the days after the trek, I realised that the comments from the trekkers and the engagement we'd created really made my adventure more enjoyable. It was like we were on a trek with a few thousand people—that was a pretty cool feeling.

One of the best parts of having so much Wi-Fi for me was the daily live videos we did. I'd turn on Instagram and go 'live' without the boys being aware, I loved ambushing them with this. One of the funniest moments was at the village of Tengbouche, when Nick, who was suffering from the 'Khumbo Cough,' which occurs with the drying of the lungs from the cold winds, was sitting in the sun with a lemon, honey, and ginger tea—he looked the worse for wear. I was sitting next to Larry; we were about 10 metres away from Nick. I quietly said to Larry, to go to YouTube and load the song 'Walking on sunshine' by the group 'Katrina and the Waves'. As Larry loaded it and hit play, I went live on Instagram and had whispered to the viewers to 'watch this' and turned the camera onto Nick, who realised a little too quickly for my liking what we were up to. Nick started to dance from a seated position, as he did the laughing faces started streaming up the face of the page, clearly everyone else saw the same humour in this that I did.

I laughed so much that I thought that I would pee my pants. It was times like this that having social media when you are deep into a trek is a good thing, it really helped people feel that they were a part of this adventure with us.

The day arrived that we would walk to Everest Base Camp. We woke up early at the village of Lobouche, and it was cold! It was close to minus 25 degrees Celsius inside our room! As we departed, we looked up the glacier to be shown where Base Camp was, it didn't seem too far into the distance, but Shiva was adamant that it would take us until mid-afternoon to reach it. It seemed incomprehensible—the distance didn't

Looking up at Mount Everest and looking down to Everest Base Camp, standing on the edge of the Khumbo Glacier

seem that far. The reality is that when you are walking at an altitude of over 5000 metres (which is more than double the height of the highest point of Australia), you are moving very slowly. Even the smallest incline takes a significant effort.

We arrived at the village of Gorekshep at around 10am, dropped our packs and had an early lunch. At that point we were all on the local noodle soup. It was warm, and it was delicious, and it didn't leave you with that heavy feeling you get in your stomach when you start walking again. What it didn't do however, was give you the sustenance that a larger meal would, but that's where we supplemented the soup with chocolate bars.

Having departed Gorekshep for Base Camp we passed some of the people we'd met along our journey. They had already been to our destination and were heading back to rest in the tea house. There was a lot of excitement from them, so we gathered that it must be pretty special to see—it didn't disappoint.

As we approached, we stood on the edge of the Everest Glacier, looking to where Base Camp sits inside an enormous white rocky outcrop, nestled on the ice. Shiva stopped us and pointed, saying to me, 'it's just there, can you see it?' Here I was looking for people and prayer flags that look like bunting, but I couldn't see what he was excited to show me. I told him that I couldn't see, and he pointed once again, 'over there, you can see the people, there is someone in a red jacket'. Now I know that I'm a little short sighted, but my eyesight isn't that bad. I looked and looked and then all of a sudden, following his pointing arm, I saw the tiniest red blob. 'Over there?' yes, he replied, 'Holy crap Shiva! Noting how far we've come that looks hours away', I was deflated, but also inspired to get there.

For the next thirty minutes we walked along the edge of this enormous glacier, it seemed never ending, but the people that we could see were getting bigger as we approached. Morale which should have been bursting at this point, still hovered pretty lowly, even to the point we started to descend into the glacier. As we walked into the glacier itself, we still couldn't see the one thing that we knew signified that we were there: the large rock with 'Everest Base Camp 5364m'. Then and only then would we feel that we'd made it. Then it happened, as quickly as anything; we crossed a small rocky ledge, I saw prayer flags flapping in the freezing breeze, a few more steps and I saw a group of people taking photos in front of that rock. My mood shifted like never before.

As I saw it, I turned to look for the boys who were following. They could tell by my look of excitement, I watched their expressions change upon seeing mine, and change again to sheer adulation when they too saw the rock—We'd made it to Everest Base Camp! We were standing at the foot of the tallest mountain in the world.

We spent an hour at Base Camp, where we laughed, we joked, we hugged one another, telling each other that we'd done it. Compared to other human endeavours, we'd achieved very little but coming from an Australian summer into a Nepalese winter, having never really walked at these altitudes, to us this was special. Especially for me, who as the face of a trekking company has had so much illness in the last 18 months; for me personally, this was huge.

I had in some way conquered my own self-doubts and my own levels of internal discomfort. The thing for me was that I know every metre of Kokoda, I know when to walk hard and when to back off. I see clients filled with concerns of the unknown and not knowing what's coming, they don't know if to push or not; this was how I was on this trek. I had never seen this trek, so I didn't know what I didn't know. I loved that feeling, the feeling of experiencing something for the first time, I knew that I wanted to experience that feeling again and again and again.

Standing in Base Camp, we all took ourselves away from the group at various times to have space and think without distraction. For me, I know that for the hard-core Adventurers out there, this wasn't the culmination point as it was for us on this day, this was where their expeditions began. I walked to look at the next section to be undertaken to tackle the mountain—

that is straight up the glacier into the Khumbo Ice Fall. I stood there picturing what it would look like in peak climbing season, imagining all of the tents, the people filled with hopes, dreams, and aspirations of reaching the top, imagining them heading up and down this ice fall.

I thought of the Sherpas who are so reliant upon trekkers and climbers to provide for their families, to send their kids to school, to put food on their table and the other living costs, like medical treatments. I know that being a porter on Everest is an extremely dangerous job, paying well for the daily dangers that they face, but wondering if it was worth it. Was it worth it? I don't know. I have seen documentaries where they interview the families of the Sherpas and the absolute concern they have for the welfare of their loved ones. They're the ones who day in and day out take the most extreme risks for the welfare of their clients, some of whom treat them appallingly.

I imagined Hillary and Tenzing standing here victoriously with their expedition team. Then I thought of all of the people who have come back through this place filled with shattered dreams, the injured, the dead. Never in my life have I stood in one place that would cross such an extreme range of emotions. Where else in the world other than a church could you stand where people celebrate, commiserate, and mourn?

It was only four years earlier that 22 people were killed when an avalanche tore down the very ice fall that I was looking into. This would see the closure of the spring trekking season for the first time in 41 years. I took all of this in and realised that even though we were relatively safe, in reality, anything can happen in this environment; I was in awe of nature and acutely aware of how precious life is.

The people I had seen along my journey were no different to us. While we had different lives, cultures, and ways of providing for our families, fundamentally we are all the same. We all want to be safe; we all want to be with the ones that we love, with something to eat and somewhere to feel safe and sleep at night. No matter who we are, we all want to go home when our work is done. My job wasn't done. I had to get safely back down and safely off the Lukla runway before I would be happy that I was safe.

Let's not kid ourselves, just weeks earlier I'd fallen on Kokoda and risked serious injury. Out of all of us, I was the most likely based on current form to injure themselves. It was a friendly reminder to take it easy.

This moment while not extreme was an important step for me on my return to health. While I was still a long way from 100% healthy, I was on my way. I left inspired to share these moments with our 100% family.

BUILDING THE
OPPORTUNITY DOOR

'Don't tell me what you're going to do,
tell me what you've done'

Don James

As I have mentioned previously, this was the quote my dad gave us all the time. While it irritated the hell out of me, amusingly, it was the one thing that was now more relevant than ever.

I never lost sight of what it was that I was trying to achieve with the business, and I had been so close to achieving it. They say the most dangerous time for any business is the survival through the first two to three years. I was twice on the point of breakthrough in this period, only to have malaria and the worst ever timed rupture of an appendix thrust me backwards, not to a catastrophic level, but I had to now work even harder to get back to the point where I felt that I was once again progressing.

In March 2020, the Kokoda trekking season was set to launch. Our first trek would be for the charity 4ASD Kids, an organisation that supports the families of children on the Autism Spectrum. This trek was seeking to raise $50,000AUD with 26 participants, our largest trek to date and a brilliant way to start what would be the brands biggest year.

Previously, our biggest Kokoda season had seen us take just over 100 participants. In 2020 our bookings were set to smash 300! Things were looking good; I had worked hard in the off season to modify the product and our processes; this would see us deliver an even more superior trekking experience with greater efficiencies. This was important to me, I never wanted to see the product diminish with greater numbers, I also didn't want it to be maintained—I wanted it continually improving. To me, there is nothing worse than seeing an organisation move away from the very thing that made you love it, only because they got too big too quickly.

I worked hard on content deliverables, and I'd set in place a rigid training program for our staff, this was up to and including our emergency evacuation procedures, this would set us apart from our competition. The booking systems were overhauled, as was the clients experience from the moment of booking. I could see the professional approach I'd demanded; I knew it would deliver a client experience not seen before.

As we finalised our preparations for the season, the world would hear of a virus, believed to have originated in China. My biggest issue at that moment was that we transit through China on our way to Nepal. I wondered what impact this would have, minimal really, as we can always change airline and fly through other locations. I didn't expect what eventuated.

Arriving in Papua New Guinea, I was subjected to heat testing to enter the country, completing documentation that stated that I had not travelled through China or any other of the newly decreed banned nations. I knew there would be an impact, but I would have never assessed the extent.

As the trek got underway, as per usual we were completely unaware of world events. I have been on the track over the years and missed many impacting world headlines, such as the Paris terror attacks in 2015. It took three days for me to catch up on this, coming back onto social media to understand the gravity of this event. This would be no different.

On day three I called the office to give an update on the trek. I was informed there was the 'slightest potential' that this would affect us; from what I knew, I didn't believe that it would. On day six I was told 'the world you left is not the one that you're coming back to'. How could this be? We'd not been out there that long, what had happened in three days? Little did we know.

We made calls the following day and came to understand that this was massive. We had the risk that people on this trek may not be able to get home. Not only was Australia going to close, but the states within it were closing too. How the hell would I get people back to places like Melbourne, Perth and the US! I have a US Citizen on the trek! Can she get home? Will she be allowed into her country? The questions that we had, only raised more questions. Even those with the most up to date news didn't know either.

What would this do to the trekking season? What would this do to all of the treks that I have paid for, in good faith for people to come within the next six weeks? Would I be able to get their monies back? What would I

Completely unaware of what was happening in the world, the 4ASD Kids Charity Trek in March 2020, just as the world began shutting down. There was a real threat we wouldn't be able to get home, the challenges of a large group were about to exponentially increase as we tried to get everyone back to Australia and the US.

be able to refund? Can I afford to refund the people that are outside of the mandatory six-week period that we set for refunds? What will this do to the business? Will we survive? I just didn't know.

What I did know is there were things that mattered, and there were things I could control. For now, all that I could control and the things that mattered were the people on this trek. I needed to have faith that the rest would sort itself out. I decided to take control by giving them all of the information that I had, not filter any of it. I wanted to make sure that I gave them such a great experience, hoping that it allowed them not to worry about the events at home; just let them enjoy themselves right now.

At one stage while we were still on the track, we were informed that Australia was closing its international border. I can assure you that this was a moment of stress—what would we be able to do? Where could we go? Would we have to wait in Papua New Guinea? We only had a thirty-day visa and we had already used close to two weeks of it. There were just so many unknowns. We gave the satellite phone to one of the clients who had a friend in the government. He came back with advice that the border would close in three days' time; we would make it—just!

We were then informed that we would all have to quarantine at home for 14 days, but what did that mean? Were we able to fly to other states? Did we have to quarantine in Brisbane, which is where we would fly into Australia? If this was the case, when we had completed quarantine, could we then travel to home states? It was still like every question was pulling a thread of questions.

These were issues that had never been considered in the history of our country. Nobody knew the answers! Governments didn't know, they were making things up daily as fast as the situation changed, it was just so fluid. What this meant to us in the travel industry was that people were desperate for us to be able to guide them, but we didn't know ourselves! When could they travel? When did we think they could travel? What happens if this happens? What happens if that happens? Much like the government, we just didn't know!

People were desperate to ask about their specific situations, and to be frank, we didn't know what we could or couldn't say, we felt like we were penned into a corner. Some people were holding us to guidance we'd given, only to have the legislation change minutes later. We were literally between the rock and the hard place.

If you are going to look for a positive in this, it's that it really took our business model to the next level. We re-wrote policies that are now watertight. Processes have been implemented that protect those clients that follow our guidance. But it's also their right not to follow this guidance too.

We made systematic changes that now see's people reminded a week prior to our 'no refund cut-off date'. This reminder affords a client the ability to cancel their booking with no financial penalty, therefore creating a better client experience. We learned that we had to remind them of these dates to protect them, and to protect us. So, if you want to look at a positive from COVID, it's that we now offer a better experience for the client with a clearer understanding of the policy and the process. That's a good thing!

The one thing that we did see with COVID is the generosity and kindness of human nature within our community. Sure, there was a percentage of people who demanded money back when legally there was no entitlement, we have been threatened with legal action, a lot. At no stage did or have we held money back from people who were entitled to it. We had some demanding refunds, when according to the legislation they were only entitled to a travel credit, this was something that we had to hold firm on.

We never like seeing people doing it tough, and while we empathised with their personal circumstances, we knew that if we started feeling sorry for them, they would lie about their situations—we saw it daily. Offering refunds to those not entitled only stood to compromise the future of the business. We never wanted to let those down who in good faith, believed and invested in us. We owed it to them to remain strong, but I know that this came across to some that we were being pricks by not giving them what they wanted, not what they were entitled to. We really saw the best and worst in people.

Admiral William H McRaven, an American four-star military officer famously gave a speech at the University of Texas where he said, 'If you want to change the world, be your best in the dark moments'. He later went on to explain that when night diving there will always be light. For a Navy SEAL to achieve their mission, they have to go to the hull of a ship, where it's the darkest and noisiest part of the ship, there is no light at all. He said, 'The darkest moment of the mission is the time when you must be your calmest, you need to remain composed—when all your tactical skills, your physical power and all your inner strength must be brought to bear'. No matter how dark a situation may be, if you want to change the world, always look for the light. This resonated with me, I could sit here looking at the dark of this situation, or I could look for the light. I chose to look for all the light that I could see

How you look for the light in this situation can be hard. We're an international travel company. We were in an environment where not only was there no international travel, for a period the 'no international travel ban' was extending daily—at one point, it was out to 2024. We knew we had to do something, but what? With people not permitted to travel internationally, in many cases they were not even permitted to travel interstate. Some were restricted to local areas and others locked in their homes for months on end. What could we do to keep people enthused and 'seeing the light'?

The one thing I was able to do was inform people of the things that I knew, and the fastest and most efficient way I could offer this information, was via Facebook! More people were using social media more frequently than ever before. If people were on their phones, I wanted to capture this. So, one Friday afternoon, I went live to our community on Facebook to at least be a face. Talking to them, letting them know about the situation we faced together, and letting them know that we weren't hiding from them, we were there!

Above all, I wanted people to see me. I wanted them to know that we hadn't run off with their money, their investment was safe, and together, we'd all get through this.

What I saw was that week to week, the number of viewers grew. People started saying hello to me and I would talk to them. For many in lockdown, I was their only human contact for the week, this became more and more obvious and more and more important. I could see from some of the comments, messages and emails I was receiving that I had to start calling people through the week as welfare checks, sometimes almost being a counsellor to them as they talked for up to two hours. I never minded, I liked the fact they felt so comfortable, but it really highlighted to me the impact that COVID was having, and the importance we played in the lives of many. It showed me that we were not only fighting for the survival of the brand for ourselves as business owners, but literally for the community. I would continue to look for the light.

GREAT SOUTHERN LAND

Survival can be summed up in three words, never give up.
That's the heart of it really, just keep trying.

Bear Grylls

Knowing there were travel restrictions gripping the country, we noticed we were able to travel to the Northern Territory. We wanted to show people we were there to inspire them. We wanted to show people the light, we wanted to show our community there were travel options, they just had to make safe travel decisions to fulfill this desire.

Knowing the Larapinta Trail in the Northern Territory is rated with Tibetan, Nepalese, European and New Zealand treks, we wanted to do it. I wanted to show people that we had options here in Australia and honestly, I wanted to at least have a look at it. I never thought we'd run treks there—I just wanted to offer the community some hope.

I made a call to a guy who ran logistics in Alice Springs, and from this conversation I quickly discovered that not only were we going to walk Larapinta, but we would also walk it with an eye to adding it as a new trek, something we could do in the uncertainty of international travel.

Larry, Nick and I travelled to Alice Springs to hit the trail, focussed on inspiring our community to come for a trek with us, but also to have a look at how we would run it.

Much like when I socialised Nepal, social media went nuts! People wanted to do it, and they wanted us to facilitate it for them, plus, we knew we had the model in place to achieve it.

When we expanded from 100% Kokoda to 100% World Wide Adventures, one of the 'sister companies' we'd created for 100% Kokoda was 100% Adventure, this would be the 'everything else' company, the one that didn't have a title, like Everest, Kilimanjaro or Kokoda, that's where this trek would live.

Here I was a guy who only a few years earlier wanted to do five to six Kokoda treks a year, was now planning to execute my fourth company in as many years.

While looking at Larapinta, we knew it had to be unique with a point of difference from the competition, it also had to have the same 100% look and feel. Most importantly, it had to have similar cultural linkages to the other

The inclusion of indigenous culture is a massive component of our treks. Here I stand proudly with Angkerle man, 100% Adventure Guide and good mate, Shane, on the Larapinta Trail.

treks we run. To us, without the culture as a part of the experience, this was just an expensive bushwalk, and we wanted it to be anything but that.

Nick went about meeting and forging relationships with local business owners, Parks and Wildlife, and the traditional owners. They were all welcoming, but cautious as they'd seen this all before. Over the coming weeks, I would send Nick back to Alice Springs on several occasions. We made a bold statement that we would run three treks that year, noting it was July and the season finishes in September. We were mocked, but when we achieved it, the local community took notice and saw that we do what we say; they started to take us more seriously, they could also see that we were different. We were men of our word. This is best explained by the local café at Standley Chasm, which is on the trail.

Nick had visited them on several occasions and met the family who run the café. They'd seen people coming in over the years, people who much like us had made promises, but here we were, only months into it, hitting the targets we'd promised.

They appeared to be pretty happy with us, inviting us to dinner as a thank you. From this, a great relationship has been forged to the point that we employ some of their family on our treks, and to facilitate cultural appreciation. The very feature we wanted from our treks was coming to fruition.

I love and am so immensely proud of our Larapinta product. This has been Nick's project and I am so impressed and proud of him. Nick thrust himself into the community, helped local indigenous families and another trekking company which is owned by a local indigenous man. The respect he's gained from this has earnt him a 'skin name', an honour usually bestowed only on men of indigenous descent.

Larapinta has quickly become our flagship trek in the entire catalogue. It has everything! A world class rating, it's in Australia, you don't need to take a lot of time away from family or off work to achieve even a part of it.

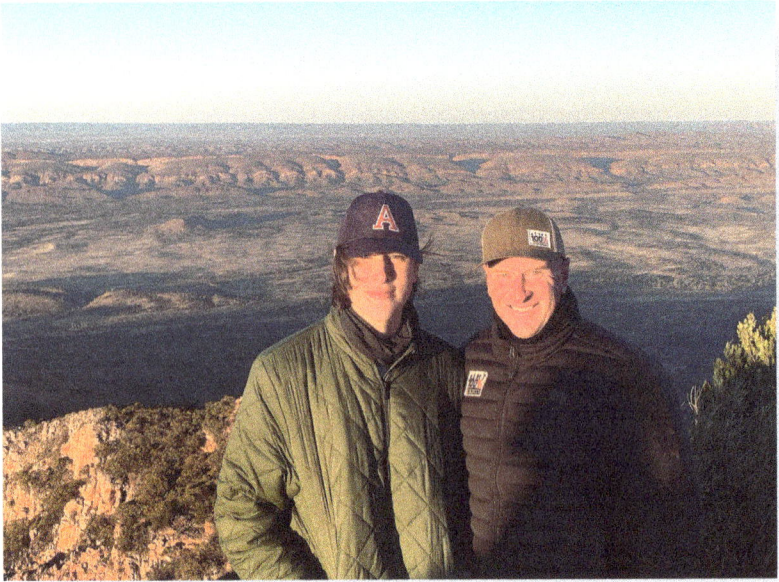

Standing with Drew at dawn on Mount Sonder, the highest point on the Larapinta Trail in the Northern Territory of Australia.

I love how we have a range of options that people can complete. People can choose from our four, seven, and 14 day packages, staying in what can only be described as a 'glamping' campsite. Each person has their own four-person sized tent in a site where the paths are lit by fire lanterns. They have a toilet, a fire pit to sit around and the meals are first class. I have seen the team make everything from lamb shanks, roasts, to vegetable frittata! People come wanting to lose weight and laugh when they feel they're putting weight on!

Trekking the Australian desert, you see colours not seen anywhere else on earth. The sunrises and sunsets are the brightest reds and oranges and at night, the desert sky is so clear that we once saw six of the eight planets all in a line with the moon. It's spectacular.

The people we've hosted on Larapinta have been the broadest cross section I am yet to see. On a Kokoda, Kilimanjaro or a Nepalese trek you will get people that are 'traditional hikers' and only a few that are curious.

On Larapinta however, there appears to be more of the curious. I believe it's the options we offer that helps those new to hiking feel comfortable and less necessity to have to walk each day like you do on the 'traditional hikes'.

On our Larapinta adventures we don't move the camp, it remains in the same place. We transport people from the camp to their start point each morning and collect them from their finish point. We then transport them back to the camp by car. What this means is that those people who seek to take a day off, can! They can sit in camp, read a book, walk to the café, and have a shower! It's these creature comforts that seem to resonate with the clientele and brought a far wider demographic to the community. I'm meeting some of the most interesting people—I love it!

Another amazing aspect of a stationary camp is that we have the local families come to meet and talk with our clients about their lives and living in remote communities. The aspect that I have found to be most inspiring is we have two men who were members of the 'Stolen Generation' come to

The Great Ocean Walk, walking the longest war memorial in the world along the Skeleton Coast of Victoria.

talk to our groups. Both Nick and I always believed the stolen generation occurred so long ago, but these men are in their early sixties! We were so wrong in our assessment.

These men discuss being taken away from their families and its moments like these on our treks that seem to have inspired our community, it's the connection they receive, the education and the country that they are walking on that has them wanting to come back time and time again to walk other sections of this trail.

With the launch of 100% Adventure and COVID travel restrictions, we knew we had to move to various parts of Australia to be able to offer treks to those that were unable in a COVID world to travel to places like the Northern Territory.

Noting we didn't know how long COVID travel restrictions would remain in place, we wanted Victoria to have an option. Victorians make up close to 50% of our clientele, and they have some amazing destinations to hike.

It didn't take us too long to look at a map and realise that Victoria is home to the longest war memorial in the world, The Great Ocean Road.

Adjacent to the Skeleton Coast is the Great Ocean Walk, a 100 kilometre walking trail that follows the headland. This seemed to us to be the logical choice, and from what we could see, there were not too many others out there offering this trek in a guided and supported package like we do.

Nick was tasked to walk it for me with the mission to come back with his idea on the best way for us to achieve this within our model. Amusingly, on the first day he twisted his knee and sat in a Victorian monsoon, but when the weather cleared, he commented that it was (as only he could say) 'stunning', and that we have to do it.

With dates planned, we set about making this trek a reality. Nick and I arrived days before the trekkers were due. We wanted to walk the two sections that he hadn't achieved on his reconnaissance—there was a COVID outbreak, and he had to cut it short. So, we each selected a section and we walked that. I departed section one, Nick drove to section two and left the keys in a lock box under the car for me. When I arrived at section two, I took the keys and drove to the end of section three to meet him for some lunch and then a drive to look at emergency travel routes. Now you are up to speed on the prologue and where this fits in—it was on this afternoon that we bogged the car for a 24 hour period.

Given a day after this to clean the vehicles, shop, pack, greet the Adventurers and brief them, we were off for what would be the first of our Great Ocean Walk treks.

To say that this trek was fun, would be under-selling it. I don't think I have laughed so much in such a short period of time. On night one, we were in the first of two campsites we use on this adventure, this one at Aire River. While sitting having a drink and a laugh with the Adventurers we could hear a noise that for many they had never heard before. For anyone who has grown up in the country, would be well aware of this noise—it was that of a mating koala, the 'ungh, ungh, ungh' sound they make is quite unique.

One of the women, Lesley, loves to take photos of wildlife. Lesley is one of the nicest people I have ever met; I met her years earlier at the Asia-Pacific Masters Games. Lesley was there to compete in Hockey, and I had a stand at the merchandising and trade expo for 100% Kokoda. Lesley had seen me there and booked a Kokoda trek.

Having trekked Kokoda with Lesley a year prior to this current trek, I had seen her intelligence and strength—I had also watched her fall over a lot too. While she'd be close to the most intelligent person in any room she was in, Lesley has a 'steely eye focus' when she see's something she wants to do or capture. On this day, I could see the ropes attaching the tents to the ground. As she launched from her chair with phone in hand to film a koala that was making its way through the camp, I yelled to her 'Lesley, watch out for the' as she face-planted into the ground to the shrieks of laughter from the remainder of the group. Determined not to miss the shot, she bounced up,

Allison, Janine, Lesley, Tracie and Samone on the Great Ocean Walk, showing Nick the way to 'Ryan's Den'.

having been on the ground for less than a second, and followed the animal across a road in the campground. Amusingly, she said 'I've never seen a koala that close before, I wasn't missing that opportunity'.

To this day, if you were to ask Tracie, Janine, Samone, Allison, Claudia, Nick or Swag, they would all laugh as they yell, 'Lesley, look out for the...'

The imagery we captured on that trek was like no other I've seen. It was as if you were walking through a lush farm in the British countryside with cows and other animals, then coming across the ocean from the most outstanding cliff top views.

One day we were walking adjacent to a paddock filled with cows, I made a comment to Allison, 'did you know that all cows are called Trevor?' She was bemused. I mentioned how years prior when cycling through the country, I was bored and called out to the cows—I called them every name, and when I called 'Trevor', every one of them turned to look at me.

I explained to her how a year or so later, I was cycling with my nephew, Blake, we came across a paddock filled with cows, I mentioned it to Blake. He didn't believe me, so I yelled 'Hey! Trevor!' and the closest cow swung its head around, Blake lost it, I thought he was going to crash.

So having explained this to Allison, she decided to give it a go, yelling 'Trevor!' to which the closest cow turned around to look at her. Laughing, she continued to ask it how it was, and asking if it is having a good day. This is the sort of fun we have on our treks; you just feel like you're with family and do silly things.

In addition to this trek, we launched a series of weekend adventure packages, one in the Bungonia National Park and the other in the Australian Alpine, within the Kosciuszko National Park. Each with benefits and each has brought about a range of things that have made me smile, laugh and wonder how I came to have this as my job.

Standing in the Bungonia National Park, overlooking the Shoalhaven River below, with Reece, Imogen, Lance, Ben, Wendy, Lainie and 'Christmas Cath'.

Bungonia is often referred to as the 'Hidden Gem' of hiking in Australia. It's nestled two hours south of Sydney and an hour north of Canberra, so it's a perfect location for a weekend away.

The thing I love about these weekends for the client is that they don't have to do anything at all—well, other than set up their esky and their bed! When I think of Bungonia I reflect upon a few things. The first is the weekend that my sister Lainie and her friends came, it would be one of the funniest weekends I've ever had.

For one, Lainie and her friends brought with them enough booze to supply a rugby club. They arrived, launched out of the car in shrieks of laughter, grabbed a big esky, ripped open the top of a bag of cheese Twisties and then the first of many bottles of Champagne, and Rosé; fixing their bedding was an afterthought! That weekend we happened to have a mate of mine, Lance, he came to cook. Lance, a professional chef of over 30 years thought this was amazing. Our camping trailers have the ability to maintain 10 people for 7 days, so with a four-burner barbeque, three hot plates, an 80-litre fridge and a 100-litre esky, all filled with fresh produce, to say the chef in him was excited was an understatement.

One of our Adventurers was Reece, an amazingly intelligent and fit man. Reece came on a Bungonia weekend with his wife, Imogen, who follows a vegan diet—Reece most definitely does not! Reece saw this as a weekend where he could consume as many meat and dairy products as humanly possible, which he did! I reflect on one conversation with his wife when she proclaimed, 'Reece, that's your third bowl of carbonara, what about the others?' A quick look at the others who were downing cheese and crackers, washed down with a bottle of their finest and he took another scoop of pasta goodness. To be fair, there was more than enough for everyone to have at least three bowls.

I will always remember Karen, my sister's friend perched on her deck chair, a glass of bubbles in one hand and a book in the other. Earlier that day as the team set off, Karen was walking towards the back of the group. This is where the joy of this program really welcomes people of all abilities. Karen had not long before had surgery, so after two hours, she announced that she'd walked enough for the day. The program at Bungonia has something for everyone, Karen had walked approximately seven kilometres when we escorted her back to the camp. When offered a cup of tea, she pointed at her esky and said, 'you go, I'm fine', and with that, poured a glass, sat down in the sun, and reached for her book.

About two hours later the next group declared that they too had walked enough for the day, so they made the short walk back to camp, only to be joined another hour after that by the final group. They started out as one, but they all took detours to get from this experience what they wanted. This is what I love about Bungonia, nobody has to walk further than they want to, and everyone can have a relaxing weekend away, one where they are both catered for and waited on.

On the walk back to camp that day, Nick had briefed the Adventurers they were walking through what he described to be the 'koala zone'. It's known to be the home of a large proportion of the local koala population. A group of people walking in the other direction, also received the same guidance from him, passing back through our camp to thank Nick—they'd seen many koalas.

The following morning, with the promise of koalas in the 'koala zone', I have never seen so many people walk so far for so long looking up! They were all on the hunt for a koala. Nick ducked away as we stood at one of the lookouts, he wanted to see if he was able to find any—the fact that he had 'guaranteed' that they would see them didn't help his cause.

After a failed attempt to spot the animal and on the receiving end of much mocking, he lent into me at the morning tea stop and said, 'I can't explain what I am doing, but can you take the next session, I have to go and do something'. Curious, yes, trusting, also yes, and without another question, I took the group down to the river so they could have a swim and take in another perspective of the National Park.

On our return close to two hours later, I walked back into camp to see a smiling Nick, proclaiming that he had in fact found koalas, and that he had one for everyone. Curious again, I burst out laughing as did the group when he opened a package that contained a chocolate 'Caramelllo Koala' for each of them.

I also laugh when I think about the random guy camped adjacent to us on another Bungonia weekend. I had once again broken a bone in my foot, this time the result of a martial arts training accident. While unable to walk, I was still able to contribute with cooking, cleaning, and hosting duties. The Saturday was hot, and the team would have been hiking for at least two hours when I decided to get started on the bolognaise I was preparing for their evening meal. As I had my things laid out, the random camper walked into our camp and up to me, 'I just saw your friends...' with a long silence. I was thinking 'random...ok...' when he said, 'they said that you'd be busy and that you could use a hand; what do you need me to do', piss off was what I thought initially, but out of my mouth came, 'I'm ok thanks, I have it all under control', all the while thinking 'Brad!!' knowing exactly who it was, my mate and business partner in 100% Adventure, Brad. He is always one for a practical joke, and this was one of his better ones. You should have seen the Cheshire cat like smile on his face when I saw him later that day.

What eventuated that day was filled with Adventure! The temperature was expected to get into the 40s.

One of the key aspects of our treks is safety, we have a rigid set of safety protocols, and everyone is briefed on what's expected. Anyway, on this day the park was quite busy—there seemed to be people everywhere!

As per our usual schedule, we were up and out the door quite early. We had the team around the top of the escarpment and heading down into the gorge to the water in good time.

As I wasn't walking, I could see other groups preparing to begin their hikes. Many looked to be lacking the necessary provisions for that day.

I always state to our teams, there will be two times when things go wrong, that is, when you're ready and when you're not, so you always have to be ready. Unfortunately for many of these people, it was quite obvious to me that they weren't ready.

As expected, just as the heat of the day started to take effect, our team began the long gorge walk, passing over the rocks and through the many water holes. I received a radio call from the team, advising me they'd come across a hiker that had fallen headfirst between two large boulders, they had a spinal issue. A moment later, I received another radio call advising me that there was by chance a doctor on the scene, and between this doctor and us, we had two satellite phones. The doctor was calling the emergency services.

Now at this point, we didn't know that the New South Wales Police Rescue Service was in the area; they were setting up to do another activity, they were now going to rescue the fallen trekker.

It was at this time as you can normally begin to expect that things started to happen with even more haste. With the heat of the day increasing, many of the un-prepared groups started to have issues with heat management, water was in limited supply, and many had failed to take sufficient provisions for the conditions—one man taking 600 millilitres of water for a day's hiking in that heat!

If you know anything about walking in the heat, you can expect to sweat close to two litres an hour! This man was a walking dehydration experiment and would need immediate assistance before he became the next person requiring an evacuation.

This is where were started to get quite frustrated with the un-preparedness of the other groups of people. In the desire to ensure that everyone in the park was having a good experience, Brad, as an act of good faith walked an hour up hill, with a good deal of haste; he needed to get greater provisions for the people in the gorge.

Having already shared a lot of the water that our group was carrying, he was at the point that he needed to take back as much water as he was able to carry. The issue, sitting and waiting for him in the heat was causing these people the need to drink even more. This would mean that Brad had to take enough water for those in the gorge, including our people, who had handed their own water supplies to the other groups. In addition, they would all need sufficient water to get themselves back out of the gorge!

I observed the Ambulance service driving past. They were unsuccessfully trying to radio the Police Rescue Team. With our team in the vicinity, I radioed our guys and had messages passed between the two, we became their 'relay'.

With our group now making their way out of the gorge with sufficient provisions, they came across a couple, clearly dis-orientated and needing assistance. The man in the pairing was in the initial stages of heat stress.

The team radioed and asked me for assistance. They'd advised the pair that their safest option was to walk back down the hill to the water filled gorge, allowing the man to sit in the water, cool his core temperature, prior to ascending the hill in the cooler late afternoon temperatures. The problem in helping this couple, was that our team had to offload even more of our

Inside 'slot canyon' in Bungonia National Park

water supplies, so yet another load of water had to be delivered. We had no options left.

I turned to the Ambulance, who had a crate of water in their vehicle. Having heard my conversation over the radio, they opened their door and handed me eight litres of water. Having already stashed cans of soft drink in an esky with chips and other salty snacks, I grabbed a bucket that I had in the back of the car, filled it with water, ice, and cans of drink, filled a day pack with food and headed off down the hill—with a broken bone in my foot, and wearing thongs. (once again, for those of you that don't understand, I was wearing 'flip flops').

Because of the swelling in my foot, I was unable to wear a shoe, my foot wouldn't fit in it—even if it did, the pain would have been too excruciating.

As I walked the first section of the trail, I began to see other un-prepared trekkers making their way out of the gorge, the looks of confusion were a mix of disorientation from the heat, combined with a lack of physical preparedness, and the sight of me, a guy in a pair of thongs, walking downhill carrying a bucket.

The walk took me forty minutes down some pretty steep and unstable terrain, sliding on the loose gravel sections, the pain emanating from the top of my foot with every step. With every slip, the pain was almost unbearable.

As I turned one of the switch back corners, I looked to the right and could see our team standing in the shade waiting for me; there was no point in them walking more when they needed more supplies. They looked happy to see me, somewhat confused by the bucket, but the looks of confusion changed when they saw I had water. This turned to happiness when they saw I had icy cold cans of Coke, and they almost screamed with delight when they saw that I had a day pack filled with chips, nuts and lollies.

With an uneventful climb out of the gorge, we arrived back to the air-conditioned comfort of my car. We spoke with the Ambulance officer about the situation in the gorge, he told us that one of the Police Rescue Team had also succumbed to a heat injury while rescuing the injured trekker.

The Kosciuszko National Park weekends in the Australian Alpine have proven highly popular. They're the perfect mix of hiking and socialising in a stunning part of the country.

The frustrating thing for us was that we had planned our trek and we intended to trek our plan. It was through the actions of others outside of our group that we had to amend our plan several times that day. Our clients saw the safety we have in place, and they saw our ability to adapt to an evolving situation. In addition to a satellite phone and a radio, our Guides carry Automated External Defibrillators, and we have another in the camp.

The following day we heard that there had been 14 rescues. We wondered how many more there would have been without Brad coming to their aid with greater supplies. In total, we offloaded 20 litres of water to people not in our group. It goes to show you that failing to prepare, really is preparing to fail.

Another weekend adventure we created is in the Kosciuszko National Park. This is one of my favourites.

Much like our other weekends, Kosciuszko is one of those places that you instantly fall in love with. I love the 'outdoorsy' feel to the town. The support network to the area is the outdoors; it's not a mining or a farming community, it's an outdoor community, and this is what this destination is to me.

Jindabyne is filled with ski, hiking, bike, and adventure stores. When you go to Thredbo in the winter, its car parks are full of cars covered with skis and snowboards. When you're there in the warmer months, there seem to be even more cars and they're covered in mountain bikes!

We camp in a local campground; I love the fire pit. There is nothing more cathartic than sitting around a fire with a drink and relaxing—it's heaven. Even though you're hiking for a good portion of the day

Stopping at Blue Lake on our way to the summit of Mount Kosciuszko, Australia's highest mountain, with Donna, Brad, Maria, myself, Lesley and Anne.

above 2000 metres in elevation, it's not too taxing. I love walking on the highest points of the country, and I love getting the chairlift down to Thredbo—it brings back so many fond memories for me being there to ski in my younger years.

One of the best moments I've had on this adventure was being with a small group. We chose to hire an onsite cabin over camping. Together we cooked, washed, and sat around eating snacks as we shared a drink. We took the chairlift up and back down to Thredbo—walking to the summit of Kosciuszko. We explored the areas around Seaman's Hut, which is on the front side of the mountain. We took photos, eating lunch as we sat in the sun surrounded by the snow.

Descending the chairlift into the village, we decided to sit in the afternoon sun at the Thredbo Pub, eating hot chips with a beer.

While not filled with the heights of adventure, it was perfect! We laughed, we hiked, and we just enjoyed one another's company. It was close to the perfect weekend, it felt to me that I was on a weekend away, not at work. This brings me back to the saying; 'find something you love, and you'll never work another day in your life'

THE FAMILY

'Family means no one gets left behind or forgotten. My family is my strength and my weakness. Without a family, man, alone in the world, trembles with the cold. The bond that links your true family is not one of blood, but one of respect and brings joy in each other's life.'

Unknown

Within my business model I was driven to create a community—a family. I never wanted a client to feel like a transaction. I wanted each person to feel as though they had joined something great.

In the early years when the structure of the brand was a lot smaller than it is today, and when I had more time, I ran Kokoda training camp weekends. What these entailed was people who were booked with us came along for a meet and greet (read nibbles and drinks) on the Friday night. This led into a brief on what they could expect from their trek and the process of how they would get to the hotel, the trail and a day by day run down. Knowledge promotes strength was my reasoning.

I invited anyone who'd previously trekked with us to come along for the Friday night activity. A lot came, even if it was just for the drinking. It was a great way to catch up with old friends, and to meet the new clients. The new clients would see groups of people laughing and socialising—many of whom had never trekked together, but had previously met at other similar events. It was like the new clients had been invited to a reunion!

I always had previous Adventurers talk about their experience. I asked them to explain what their trepidations were prior to going, the reality of the adventure, plus I asked them to offer their best tips to the group. For the ladies, this was things like sanitation, the style of pants they wore, be it shorts, leggings or tights. For the group, it was about the porters, the villages, the meals etcetera. What it did, was welcome them into the community and make them feel they had in fact joined something so much bigger than they realised. I knew their names, I knew which trek they were on, and I knew who they would be trekking with, it created some amazing introductions.

This is what I wanted; I wanted the community feel. This was never so evident as when we brought two of the porters to Australia as a reward for their outstanding service. The weekend the porters arrived, we had people fly in from all around Australia to come and see them. We took them to the rugby league in Brisbane on Friday night, and to the Gold Coast on the Saturday, which entailed beers, Teppanyaki and the Casino!

People were almost demanding in some instances to come. They came from all around the country at their own expense, paying for flights, accommodation, and entertainment—all to catch up with two guys from PNG they spent a week with—it blew my mind!

The impact of the family has proven itself time and again. I would think of Shane, who came on a trek with a mate. While he was reserved, he had a lot to offer. He didn't engage much, but he listened a lot. He seemed distant, would come into the group, but would then extract himself and do his own thing.

On about day five, he opened up, telling me about the demons that have driven his life, and how angry life made him at times. He said, 'I have never told anyone this stuff, I have never felt so comfortable, I don't know what it is—I guess, I just feel safe'.

As the trek continued, he opened more and more. Upon the completion of his trek, he gave me a hug and told me he would see me later. Normally when someone says this to me, I see it as a 'goodbye', but on this day, I literally saw it as 'I'll see you again soon', I knew we would.

Since that fateful day, Shane has become part of the fabric. He has been on two other treks, has booked to come on two more. His wife spoke to me once and said that her husband went on a trek with us, but the man she married came home—that was a powerful message.

When I think of others who have had similar feelings on a trek I think of Tracie, who once felt so safe that she opened up and told me things that she'd never told anyone in her life. She discussed toxic relationships, her children and fractures that had formed between them. She told me of her fears and her dreams.

I let her talk for about an hour. When she finished, I thanked her for feeling so comfortable to discuss this with me. She looked horrified, realising what she'd just done, almost in disbelief she'd just told me things that as she said, she'd never told another living soul, saying, she just felt so comfortable, which I guess was cathartic for her.

I'm not arrogant enough to believe that people in these situations are comfortable with me, I am the driver of the vehicle that's making them comfortable. People feel comfortable within their surroundings, which to me is amazing. I wanted a community, I never believed that this level of comfort would be one of the most powerful things to come from it.

On a similar line, I love those who come back on different adventures with us. Amusingly I see these people more often than my blood family! This is why I feel as though they are a part of my family, we spend time together in the rawness of the outdoors, we bond, we laugh, and we cry together, we share the hardships; it's bonding! I want to share some of their stories with you.

Kate is an amazing lady, in her sixties and from a large family. To date, I have taken Kate across Kokoda twice, once in each direction, the second time she came with her cousin Janine, we will get to her soon. Kate had bookings to both Nepal and Africa delayed due to COVID. In Nepal she was coming with Janine, her daughter and a grandchild.

Kate has been to Kosciuszko with us, and she's booked to come on the Great Ocean Road. Kate was set to do our 2021 full-length

Larapinta adventure. With husband Allen, they were literally hours from getting in their car to drive from Victoria, taking a road trip with their caravan to the Northern Territory. This trek was also taken away from her thanks to a COVID travel restriction. Devastated, she has booked to come back next year as a member of a different group, with people with whom she has previously trekked Kokoda. This is what I mean about this community we've created; it just keeps re-bonding itself. I love it!

The other exciting thing for Kate, is that Allen is becoming more and more involved. Not physically up to the rigors of trekking himself, he was set to travel to Tanzania while Kate was trekking Kilimanjaro, he'd meet her there to participate on the Safari component at the completion of the trek.

I love that we have this ability to include other members of the family who can't or don't wish to trek. Allen, a bit of a dab cook, will be the Camp Chef on Kate's Larapinta, this is what it's all about. He will be an integral member of the community, without ever walking on a trail. He'll earn his own 100% 'coins' (which is what each participant earns for completing a trek, either as a client or on staff), this means he can partake in the games that we play with the coins. I just love that we can include everyone, trekking or not.

Janine is Kate's cousin. Much like Kate, she has found a family with us, one that's external to her own. A former professional dancer and coach, Janine is a fit lady. She came to Kokoda with a mental image of how she'd successfully cross the range. What eventuated however was a vastly different picture, a picture she didn't quite understand until her second trek, the Great Ocean Walk.

It was on this walk that I was able to spend a lot more time with Janine. I was facilitating the logistics, which meant I was more mentally present, and able to talk to her with a lot greater scope than I can on a Kokoda trek.

To explain, when guiding on Kokoda, I will get at best half an hour a day with each adventurer. The reason is that I must check on everyone, but I also have a trek to manage. I have to make sure that each of the porters is in the right place at the right time for the trek to be seen as seamless.

That is—who has the safety equipment? Where are they now? Where is the chef? Where is he stopping for lunch? What's he preparing, and has he considered those with dietary preferences and allergies? What's the condition of the trail? Are there any obstacles that could change our passage? Where's the lead man? Am I able to call out to him or do I need to run ahead? Who is struggling and who is having an easy day? How much do I separate people, so we all arrive at the same place at the same time? This is an example of some of the things I have running through my head while I walk on Kokoda.

You can start to see that this in your head all day means that even when you're talking to someone, at times, you're not listening as intently as you want to, you're always observing the conditions and predicting to prevent a possible safety issue.

On the Great Ocean Walk however, I had the time to talk to Janine with greater focus and no mental distraction. She mentioned how she loved Kokoda, but it didn't go as well as she thought it would. It was at this time I became aware of the image she'd painted for herself, and how it was so far removed from the reality that unfolded. She wasn't the adventurer she believed she'd have been, saying 'I struggled', I laughed.

You may be wondering why I laughed, let me explain to you as I explained to her that day.

Janine was comparing herself to the single group she trekked with. I was comparing her performance on Kokoda against the hundreds of people that I have seen cross the trail. Janine happened to find herself in a group that contained some elite athletes, such as a current Australian trail running champion, former soldiers, a physical training instructor who came with clients that he'd trained for the adventure. There was another man of Janine's vintage and of course, her cousin.

On a trek of 14 people, she was in her view in the bottom three. I mean why wouldn't she have been, they were all fit! Even when compared to a cross section of society, they were fit—that's a hard gauge to assess yourself against.

I showed her that on any of the other nine treks I facilitated that year, she would have been with the fittest and the fastest. As I explained to her, she was in effect in an Olympic final, disappointed with a seventh placing.

Janine led the group the following day, arriving in camp close to thirty minutes ahead of the others. Her face had a look of understanding to what I'd said to her the day prior, it not only filled my heart, but it made me so proud of her. I will never forget the look of pride on her face as she finally believed in herself the way that I believed in her. It shows the power of psychology, that when someone believes in themselves the way that I believe in them, they break the lock of their own performance and perform to the picture painted in their minds.

Janine has since booked to come to Larapinta and has just completed the Great Ocean Walk for a second time. She epitomises what I want to

We love 'the family.' All returning Adventurers, with Mim, Cathy, Maria and Tracie with myself, Brad, Jordie and Nick kneeling on a Kosciuszko Weekend.

achieve with this brand, she trusts us, and she believes in the product. Most importantly to me, like with Shane and Tracie, it's her 'safe place'.

Another lady who came on a trek filled with self-doubt was Samone. Samone came to Kokoda excited, anxious, and as bad as this will sound, as it's something I see a lot, she was a woman that came from a relationship that appeared supporting, but when you get into the weeds of it, was anything but.

Samone, much like Janine, had an image in her mind of what her adventure would look like. The difference with Samone is that her adventure unfolded a lot closer to what she'd predicted. Where it differed however, was the confidence and self-belief she took away from it.

Empowered, she started as a self-titled 'wife/mother/housekeeper', completing her trek with the title of empowered woman! She'd arrived! She left Kokoda that day a self-confident woman who believed in herself, as a contributing member of a team—a team that relied upon her as much as she relied upon it.

One of my most fond memories of Samone is a photo I have of her and some of the other women on that trek, taking a 'selfie' at the Kokoda airfield with a beer in one hand and their 'I completed Kokoda coins' in the other. The next lasting memory for me is when I saw her months later, arriving for her Great Ocean Walk. In walked a woman filled with pride and confidence to greet me, not the woman I'd met months earlier, who sheepishly said hello. Here was a woman who had the greatest gift any woman can have— self-belief! It remains one of my fondest memories of the brand, and it has literally nothing to do with hiking.

For me it's about the people I meet and being able to learn their story. I clearly recall the night I met Kelly.

Hosting a training weekend in my hometown, I remember standing in the bar of the hotel where we hosted the event. I remember watching a man and two ladies walk around the corner. The man, Mark, attended that night with his wife, Julie, and their friend Kelly.

After basic introductions, Kelly seemed happy enough, but had a look of concern/apprehension/trepidation on her face. I was curious, to me, she didn't have the 'excited to be there look' you'd normally see in these situations.

With the arrival of the final guests, we moved into the conference room for a series of briefs. I had the desks in a 'U' shape facing a screen. As I stood facing the group, Kelly was to my immediate left, second from the end—a childhood friend, Karl, sat next to her on the end. Having introduced myself, and briefed the scope of the night, I asked each participant to introduce themself and why Kokoda; that is, what's the picture in their head of this experience, and what's their inspiration for doing it. In looking towards Karl to introduce himself, Kelly moved her hands to the top of the desk, the light from her wedding ring hitting me in the face, curious a married woman was coming with a couple, and without her husband.

Karl finished his introduction, we all looked to Kelly for her turn. My perception of the human story was about to be changed.

Kelly began by saying that she'd never held a desire to walk Kokoda. I was curious, she told us that her husband however had, I was now even more curious to why he wasn't here. She then went on to tell us how he'd recently passed away from illness, she'd promised him in the lead up to his death that she'd complete both of their bucket list travel destinations. Kelly mentioned how her good friends Mark and Julie were coming to Kokoda to help her tick this item from her husband's list.

I stood there with nothing to say in reply, normally I'm able to say something, but I stood there in shock that such a young woman had such a sad story. I welcomed her and said that I would do everything within my power to make it the most amazing experience for her.

Kelly's one of those people, that when she talks, you learn. For a woman in her thirties, she's met, married, and farewelled the love of her life. She's travelled to over fifty countries and wants to travel to at least fifty more, she is an inspiration and the type of person you could expect to meet on our treks. Kelly is a great example of how you never know the paths someone's walked to get to this point.

In the years that followed that night, I've spent many weeks with her. Like Shane, she's become a part of the fabric of the company, walking and now working on our adventures. I love talking with Kelly and learning more about her life and her travels. She's one of the people I could listen to for hours, she has done some of the most amazing things and seen parts of the world I never knew existed. She has an amazing story.

It's people like Kelly that make me love what I do so much, I get to meet and learn from such remarkable people. These are the people I think about when I seek inspiration, it's these people that make me want to strive to be better in my own life. I will never forget the night that I met her—I am a better man for it.

Just one year prior to the night I met Kelly, I met Allison, who was booked to come to Kokoda with a friend and two of her children.

I laugh when I think about how Allison and I came to meet. Allison had been camping with friends. One of these friends, Mez, won the competition I ran when I launched the business.

As is pretty common, camping comes with drinking, Mez had said to Allison 'I won a trek and am doing Kokoda, you should come!' OK replied a tipsy Allison, who then declared that two of her kids would come too! She booked for the three of them, and the rest is history!

Allison not only came to Kokoda with children Callum and Claudia, but she sent Callum back the following year to trek with another of her kids, Zach. Allison was on one of the first three Larapinta treks we ran in 2020. Later that year, along with Claudia, she came to Bungonia, both backing up to be on our first Great Ocean Walk. Allison came to Bungonia for a second time in 2021, this was as a reunion with the women she met on the Great Ocean Walk. She's also booked to come to Kosciuszko with us. This totals 12 treks she's bought from us. She's been a magnificent supporter of our brand and been there to help us as much as we try to help her. I laugh at her quote about trekking with us, where she said, 'I feel like I'm going on holiday with my naughty brothers'.

In a conversation with Allison and Claudia on the Great Ocean Walk, it was mentioned that Claudia, who was entering her final year at high school, didn't know what she wanted to do as a profession. I laughed and offered for her to come and work with us! She's a great young woman who can cook, drive, clean, chop wood and do so much more! I figured with us, she'd get paid to get some life experience and could take a year to see what she wanted to do from there. She may stay, who knows!

The family really shone through most recently when on the night prior to a Larapinta, as per usual we had dinner with the Adventurers. That night at dinner however, we had three additional guests, Shane, his wife Sharon and their grandson, Parker. We all laughed and joked and enjoyed a great night together.

We introduced everyone, though the clients about to embark on their adventure couldn't quite work out how Shane and his family fit into our dynamic. The following morning, having had photos with Parker, we said our farewells to the family to commence the trek. The Adventurers asked once again who they were and how they were aligned to the brand. They smiled when we explained how Shane was once a client, but now works for us, he's a part of our logistics team. His wife and grandson came to spend time with him, and by proxy, us too. They saw the community, but it was about to become even more prominent, even more so for us too.

That evening, having completed the days trekking and preparing dinner, a van pulled up in our camp. Out of the van stepped Lisa and her friend Kylie. Lisa is a former client as well, and amusingly, knows Kate and Janine having trekked Kokoda with them.

Lisa was meant to complete Larapinta two weeks prior, but due to a COVID travel restriction, was unable to arrive in time for the commencement of her trek. She was however free to travel to the Northern Territory a week later. Along with her friend Kylie, they planned to meet up at the completion of Lisa's trek, intending to travel to Uluru, Kings Canyon and the surrounds. Thanks to COVID, if she couldn't complete both the trek and her follow-on travel plans, she was determined to do as much as she could.

Lisa and Kylie knew where we were, they'd come and stayed with us a week prior, we took them on a Larapinta day trip. We were so thrilled that they came back! They wanted to come and say goodbye before they headed home to Melbourne.

As they stepped out of their van, there was so much joy and excitement. The Adventurers on the trek were once again confused who yet another group of people were.

Having introduced them all, we explained who Lisa and Kylie were and asked them if they wanted dinner, offering them to park their van in the camp that night. They excitedly agreed that they would.

Together that night they shared the campfire with the Adventurers. Laughing and getting along so well they exchanged details and arranged to come on a trek together. This is what the family is to us. It's moments like this that show us that we created a community, a 'tribe' if you will. We had completed what we set out to achieve in that people don't feel like a transaction, they feel they've joined something far greater than any individual purchase.

What each of these people have in common—be it Shane, Tracie, Kate, Janine, Samone, Allison, Lisa and even Lesley, is they have all been instrumental in the survival of our brand through COVID.

COVID took us to the brink of survival. Nick and I worked hard, and we had to work fast in such a dynamically changing environment—we had to maintain the existence of the brand. At times it was tough; but we had to keep smiling and give people the same stability we always had. Any of these people were entitled to take their deposited funds back, and with the COVID refund policy, they were all entitled to do so—but not one of them did. Rather than take back their money, they each chose to invest in the brand, and by proxy, they invested in us!

There were some very tough times and some tough conversations between Nick and I. Above my desk (and I just looked at it in writing this) is a receipt which on the back of it has written 'We are mates as a priority, this comes first!' We both signed it as our 'contract' to one another.

It was this receipt through COVID we both had to fall back upon. Just the other day he sent me a text that only said 'love ya!' When I called him, he said that we only ever talk work now; it was a beautiful moment and, in a way, COVID created it. That message meant the world to me.

Nick and I—while business partners—are mates, we were mates first and we're committed to being mates well after this is over. The belief that these people showed in us will never be forgotten.

We love when people embrace the community and the company of others as much as the adventure. Here with Donna, Tracie, Lesley, Cathy, Mim, Maria and Anne.
Anne was the only member of the group that had never been on a 100% adventure prior to that weekend.

THE FUTURE

'The future's so bright I gotta wear shades'

Song lyric by Timbuk3

I'm often asked what the number tattooed on the underside of my arm represents. The number, 30095, represents the number of days that my dad lived—he died at 82. Let me explain what this means to me.

By the time I complete writing this book, I'll be 47 years old. In days, that means I've been alive for 17155 days. If I was to live to the exact number of days as my dad, I look at it with simple math.

Let's take the 30095 days that my dad lived, subtracting the 17155 days that I've lived thus far. What this means to me, is that I'm now very aware that I only have 12940 days until my death.

Let's hypothesize and say that for the last ten years of my life, I can't do all the things that I want to—with age, I become physically limited and more sedentary. I therefore need to subtract another 3650 days (ten years) off this number. So, let's take the 12940 days that we already ascertained I have, and subtract an additional 3650 days. This means that I now only have 9290 days to achieve all the things I desire. Noting I'm living life the way I desire now; I have chosen to live every one of these precious days.

Now! If I were to hold a 'normal' job and work to the retirement age in Australia, which is currently averaged at 65 years old, this means that post retirement, I would only have seven years to do all the things I dreamt I would complete in my post career life. This would only leave me with 2555 days to live the post work lifestyle I dreamt of; I like my equation more.

I will give you another way to look at this. Almost everyone you meet has a bucket list. I do too, not that I call it a bucket list, I don't even know what I would call it. What I do know is that the term bucket refers to dying, as in 'kicking the bucket', to me that's a little morbid, and takes me back to the numbers that I just listed.

Why would I want to look at the end number and see the ticking of the clock that way, when I can look at the number as an investment and choose to live them all now.

A guy I know recently died of cancer; he socialised his entire journey. Every day I would watch his daily video journal. One day he said, 'I'm not scared of dying, dying will be the easiest thing I do, I am scared of not living well enough. I'm scared of not being there for my wife and kids'. This resonated with me, it resonated with me because it's aligned to something I'd heard—I don't recall who was the first to say it, but my dad once said it to me when he said, 'you die once, but you live every day'. This is how I want to live; I want to live every day, and this is why I don't have a bucket list, I have a 'to do list'. There you go, I just named it.

What's on my to do list? There is so much. As I mentioned earlier, I have a lot more to explore in Dubai and the UAE. I want to surf the Northern Lights in Iceland, I want to spend more time in New York and watch the basketball in Madison Square Garden, I also want to watch the New York Yankees play the New York Mets at Yankee Stadium. I want to ride my bike in France, up in the hills of the Tour de France. I want to watch the tour live. I want to go to the Monaco Formula 1 Grand Prix; I want to ride a motorbike through the Himalaya, and I want to drink cocktails looking at the sunsetting in Hawaii once again.

Sure, I have other things that I want to achieve where you can come with me. I want to hike in Iceland and swim in the thermal pools. I want to

WITH THANKS

There are too many people that I would like to and need to thank, but I would hate to offend someone by forgetting them here. For those of you I wish to thank, I will reach out to you personally—I have already started. The first person I thanked was Col, my boss from my apprenticeship. I wanted to thank him for taking a chance on and believing in me—he told me I was worth it, he made me cry, I don't believe anyone is worth what he gave me.

I would like to thank the many mentors I've had in my life, from my high school mathematics teacher, Matt Hutchison, to my former big boss in the Army and now mentor in this project, Ian Gordon. Matt educated me as much about being a man as he did about maths, and Ian, you're such an inspiring and humble man. There have been many more mentors who have contributed to my story. To those of you, I would not be the man I am today without your influence, I thank you all.

Dad always said to me, that 'everyone in life is an example, so be a good one'. If I mentioned you in this book, I thank you, and if I didn't mention you, then I really thank you. Together you have all shaped who I have become.

To Mum and the family, thank you for allowing me to dream and believe that anything was possible. While Dad wasn't here to see the most recent chapters, Mum, without you 100% doesn't exist—our community owes you so much. Dad, I am now a published author, so this is what I've done!

To Abbey and Drew, don't tell me what you're going to do, tell me what you've done.

To everyone else, I'll see you out there—Cam!

www.ingramcontent.com/pod-product-compliance
Lightning Source LLC
Chambersburg PA
CBHW051439270326
41931CB00020B/3475

hike the rim of the Grand Canyon, prior to walking through it, this comes with a trip along Route 66 and finishes in Vegas. I also want to walk Mont Blanc and pass through three countries in one hike. I want to drink sangria on part of the Camino. I want to eat a Chicken Kiev in Kiev, (I don't actually, I once dared a mate to do it and he said it was horrible), but I would love to do a home stay cooking course in Italy, like my brother and parents once did. There are so many more things I want to do.

Will I be disappointed if I don't do them all? Not one bit, because I am choosing to live now. If I don't get to them, I know that I will be busy with people much like yourself. I wonder, will we be hiking the Kokoda Trail, or through the populated and the most remote parts of Nepal. Maybe we'll be on a safari together in Africa, touring Antarctica, or walking through the Sun Gate along the Inca Trail to Machu Picchu. Maybe we'll be hiking in Argentina or in Russia. These are all things we currently do, or things I have planned to facilitate at one point in the future.

No matter what it is, I know that my dad would be proud. Before he racked up number 30095, he said 'mate, this isn't a dress rehearsal, this is the only life you'll ever get, don't waste it, get out there and live', I can say hand on heart that I am doing what he wanted, I am living every one of the days of my son's future tattoo. Until that day comes, all I'll say, is that I'm heading outside, because that's where the adventure lives, who's coming with me?